Lecture Notes in Computer Science 4623

Commenced Publication in 1973
Founding and Former Series Editors:
Gerhard Goos, Juris Hartmanis, and Jan van Leeuwen

Martine Collard (Ed.)

Ontologies-Based Databases and Information Systems

First and Second VLDB Workshops,
ODBIS 2005/2006
Trondheim, Norway, September 2-3, 2005
Seoul, Korea, September 11, 2006
Revised Papers

 Springer

Volume Editor

Martine Collard
Université de Nice - Sophia Antipolis
Laboratoire I3S
Les Algorithmes, 2000 route des Lucioles, 06903 Sophia Antipolis, France
E-mail: Martine.Collard@unice.fr

Library of Congress Control Number: 2007936205

CR Subject Classification (1998): H.2.1, H.2.4, H.3

LNCS Sublibrary: SL 1 – Theoretical Computer Science and General Issues

ISSN   0302-9743
ISBN-10   3-540-75473-3 Springer Berlin Heidelberg New York
ISBN-13   978-3-540-75473-2 Springer Berlin Heidelberg New York

Springer is a part of Springer Science+Business Media

springer.com

© Springer-Verlag Berlin Heidelberg 2007
Printed in Germany

Typesetting: Camera-ready by author, data conversion by Scientific Publishing Services, Chennai, India
Printed on acid-free paper   SPIN: 12162703   06/3180   5 4 3 2 1 0

Preface

This volume constitutes the joint post-proceedings of the two international VLDB workshops on Ontologies-based Techniques for DataBases and Information Systems, ODBIS 2005 and ODBIS 2006, co-located with the 31st and 32nd International Conference on Very Large Data Bases (VLDB). It is a collection of extended versions of papers presented at the workshops.

Ontologies are generally used to specify and communicate domain knowledge in a generic way. While in a formal sense "ontology" means study of concepts, one can use the word "ontology" as a concept repository about a particular area of interest. Ontologies are very useful for structuring and defining the meaning of the metadata terms that are currently collected inside a domain community. They are a popular research topic in knowledge engineering, natural language processing, intelligent information integration and multi-agent systems. Ontologies are also applied in the World Wide Web community where they provide the conceptual underpinning for making the semantics of a metadata machine understandable. More generally, ontologies are critical for applications which want to merge information from diverse sources. They become a major conceptual backbone for a broad spectrum of activities dealing with databases and information systems. In these workshops, the objectives were to present databases and information systems research as they relate to ontologies and, more broadly, to gain insight into ontologies as they relate to databases and information systems. These post-proceedings are divided roughly into three sections: ontology-based interoperability and schema matching, management of ontological bases and links between ontologies and knowledge.

May 2007   Martine Collard

Editorial Board

Table of Contents

A Multi-level Matching Algorithm for Combining Similarity Measures in Ontology Integration

Ahmed Alasoud, Volker Haarslev, and Nematollaah Shiri

Computer Science & Software Engineering, Concordia University
1455 De Maisonneuve W., Montreal, Quebec, Canada
{ahmed_a,haarslev,shiri}@cse.concordia.ca

Abstract. Various similarity measures have been proposed for ontology integration to identify and suggest possible matches of components in a semi-automatic process. A (basic) Multi Match Algorithm (MMA) can be used to combine these measures effectively, thus making it easier for users in such applications to identify "ideal" matches found. We propose a multi-level extension of MMA, called MLMA, which assumes the collection of similarity measures are partitioned by the user, and that there is a partial order on the partitions, also defined by the user. We have developed a running prototype of the proposed multi level method and illustrate how our method yields improved match results compared to the basic MMA. While our objective in this study has been to develop tools and techniques to support the hybrid approach we introduced earlier for ontology integration, the ideas can be applied in information sharing and ontology integration applications.

1 Introduction

The rapid increase in the number of multiple information sources requires efficient and flexible frameworks for integration of these sources. Such frameworks should provide a way for extracting, transforming, and loading data from these sources, and be represented to the user in some appropriate way. There are two major approaches for integration of information: (1) the data warehouse (DW) or materialized approach and (2) virtual approach (also called mediator based).

In the context of ontology integration, we proposed a third approach [1] which is a hybrid between fully materialized and fully virtual approaches. Fig. 1 shows the architecture of this approach. The motivation of our ongoing research on integration of source ontologies was to develop tools and techniques for situations in which the information sources are expressed as ontologies, and to support queries over these sources, we need to build the global ontology (which has a common vocabulary among the sources). This allows the query processing (QP) component in the integrated framework in Fig. 1 to extract information from the ontology sources. To support this capability and realize the architecture proposed in Fig. 1, we need to develop effective matching techniques to assist users in a semi-automatic process. This is the motivation of the current work.

Let us review the issues faced in ontology matching, which is a fundamental problem in sharing information and integrating ontology sources in numerous

M. Collard (Ed.): ODBIS 2005/2006, LNCS 4623, pp. 1–17, 2007.
© Springer-Verlag Berlin Heidelberg 2007

applications. We witness a continuous growth in both the number and size of available ontologies developed to annotate knowledge on the web through semantics markups to facilitate sharing and reusing by machines. This, on the other hand, has resulted in an increased heterogeneity in the available information. For example, the same entity could be given different names in different ontologies or it could be modeled or described in different ways. The Ontology Matching Problem (OMP) may then be described as follows: given ontologies O1 and O2, each of which describing a collection of discrete entities such as classes, properties, individuals, etc., we want to find the semantic correspondences that exist between the components of these entities.

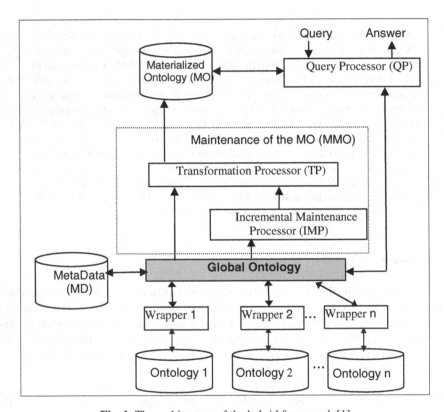

Fig. 1. The architecture of the hybrid framework [1]

Very often existing matching algorithms focus on one-to-one (1:1) matching. These methods hardly consider several entities at the same time and correspondingly use several similarity measures to solve OMP. In fact, OMP is an n:m matching problem. In order to obtain better matching results, existing measures should be used simultaneously and combined in a multi-space matching framework. We have developed such a method using a multi match algorithm (MMA).

The contributions of this paper are as follows:

1. We introduce an ontology matching approach, based on the idea of a multi-level match algorithm, in which each level uses different similarity measure(s).
2. We propose a flexible measure to compute the best possible matching state offered by MMA. This principle is based on the Dice coefficient adapted for our use.

The rest of the paper is organized as follows. In Section 2 we set up the formulation of the framework. The description of the algorithm is introduced in Section 3. An illustrative scenario is given in Section 4. The experiments and results are presented in Section 5. The related work is provided in Section 6. We conclude the paper with a summary and a discussion of future work in Section 7.

1.1 Motivating Example

In this section, we illustrate the ontology matching problem and introduce some concepts and techniques. Let us consider the following examples. Consider source ontology "S", which offers different types of electronic products. For simplicity, we consider only two products: PCs and laptops. Fig. 2 shows this ontology. As can be seen, S includes the concept *COMPUTERS* which represents *desktop* and *laptop*

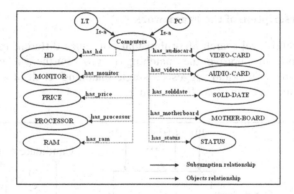

Fig. 2. Source ontology *S*

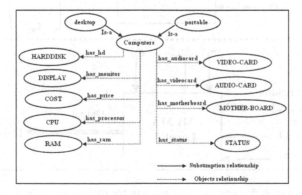

Fig. 3. Target ontology *T*

computers. Other concepts such as *MONITOR, PROCESSOR*, and *PRICE,* etc in this ontology represent technical specifications of computers. As the target ontology, we consider ontology "T", shown in Fig. 3. The goal is to find the corresponding matches among the entities in S and T.

There exist many methods to measure similarities between two entities, such as string similarity, linguistic similarity, etc. However, when we use a single matching measure for an input pair of ontologies, we may not be satisfied with the final match result. For instance, if we use a string similarity measure only, the concepts *PC* and *LT* in S have no matches in T. On the other hand, a string similarity measure is the basis for some other methods of measuring similarities between entities, and it works fine in some domains where a match in the entities on their syntax would most probably mean agreement on their semantics.

Another example is when we use a more semantic measure such as a linguistic based measure. For instance, we find out that the concept *PC* in S is mapped to the concept *desktop* in T and as well to concept *computer* in T. So, this will not help the user to focus his/her intention. As a result, if we use both measures (string and linguistic), the concept *computers* in S will be mapped into the concept *computers* in T with a very high confidence. Consequently, the concept *PC* in S will be mapped to *desktop* in T, and the concept *LT* in S will be mapped to *portable* in T.

1.2 General Description of the Framework

We propose a multi-level search algorithm that combines different measures in one unified framework to improve the matching results. Further, it minimizes user interaction with the system and suggests a single matching result of a collection of n elements in S to a collection of m elements in T.

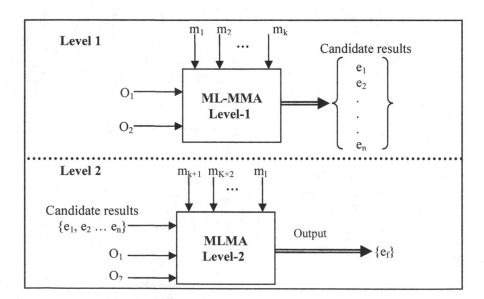

Fig. 4. A schematic description of the multi-level method

Fig. 4 illustrates the main idea of multi-level method, when there are two levels. It shows the different similarity measures $\{m_1, m_2,..., m_l\}$ divided into two, and applied at two levels.

For instance, and to ease the presentation we use three similarity measures divided into two levels. The name and linguistic similarity measures have been applied in the first level. Then, the structural similarity measure has been applied on the candidate resulting states $\{e_1, e_2 ... e_n\}$ in the second level. As a result, our method will output the state which has the highest confidence. Moreover, our resulting mapping state $\{e_f\}$ is measured based on its rich structure on one hand and the greatest number of corresponding concepts between the source ontologies on the other hand.

2 Formulation of the Framework

In this section, we provide the definitions for the main components of our framework. These definitions give the meaning of our notations such as, what are the entities we are referring to, the relationship matrix that gives the basis to compute the similarity matrix, the matching matrix, the matching space, and in the subsection we introduce the structure-based similarity measure.

We describe the mapping problem as identifying pairs of similar nodes (also called vertices) in the input ontologies modeled as labeled directed graphs. The nodes in an input graph correspond to entities in ontologies, and the edges indicate the relationships between the pair of nodes they connect. The labels indicate the kind of relationship, e.g. "domain" or "range." In this study, we limit ourselves to finding mappings for classes and relationships only.

Definition 1 (Entity-relationships). Let S be a source ontology, T be a target ontology. We use $E^S = \{s_1, s_2,..., s_n\}$ and $E^T = \{t_1, t_2,..., t_m\}$ to denote the set of entities in S and T, respectively. Entity refers to classes, properties, or individuals for which we want to find matches in the input ontologies. We use $R(r_{ij})$, defined below, to denote the relationship between entities s_i and t_j. We use r_{ij} to denote a matching degree between s_i and t_j.

Definition 2 (Relationship Matrix). This relational matrix, denoted as $R(r_{ij})$, represents the relationship between ontologies S and T, i.e., r_{ij} includes indicates the similarity between concept s_i in S and concept t_j in T. Using R, we define another relational matrix, called the *similarity matrix*, which captures a different relationship between S and T, defined as follows.

Definition 3 (Similarity Matrix). This relational matrix, denoted $L(l_{ij})$, includes entries in [0,1], called the *similarity coefficients*, representing the degree of similarity between s_i and t_j. Both R and L are n×m matrices.

Definition 4 (Matching Matrix). A matching matrix, denoted Map_{0-1}, is a 0-1 matrix with dimension n×m and with entries $r_{ij} \in \{0,1\}$. If $r_{ij} = 1$, it means that S_i and t_j are "matchable." They are unmatchable if $r_{ij} = 0$.

Definition 5 (Matching Space). All the possible assignments for the matching matrix form a *matching space*, also called the *mapping space*. Every assignment is a state in the matching space. The state represents a solution of ontology matching. The following example illustrates the above concepts and terms.

Example 1. Let S and T be the input ontologies, and $E^S=\{s_1,s_2,...,s_n\}$ and $E^T=\{t_1, t_2,...,t_m\}$ be the sets of entitie. A matching matrix Map_{0-1} indicates the similarity relation between the elements of E^S and E^T. The number of relationship matrices Map_{0-1} is $2^{n \times m}$, i.e., the matching space has $2^{n \times m}$ states. These matrices form the matching space. For instance, when Map_{0-1} is 2×2, the matching space would have 16 states. Some of these mapping states are as follows, in which the rows are entities in S and the columns are entities in T. E.g., the first matrix indicates no mapping. The third matrix below, it indicates that entity s_1 is matched with t_1 or t_2, and s_2 is matched with t_2, etc.

$$\left(\begin{bmatrix} 0 & 0 \\ 0 & 0 \end{bmatrix}, \begin{bmatrix} 1 & 0 \\ 0 & 0 \end{bmatrix}, ..., \begin{bmatrix} 1 & 1 \\ 0 & 1 \end{bmatrix}, \begin{bmatrix} 1 & 1 \\ 1 & 1 \end{bmatrix} \right).$$

2.1 Tradeoff Between Structure and Size of the Mapping States

Many similarity measures have been introduced for a set of keywords representing a text. For example, the Dice coefficient, the Jaccard coefficient, the Cosine coefficient [21], etc. The Dice coefficient is defined as follows:

$$S_{T_1,T_2} = (2|T_1 \cap T_2|)/(|T_1|+|T_2|) .$$

where $|T_i|$ is the number of terms in set T_i, and $|T_1 \cap T_2|$ is the number of common terms in T_1 and T_2. We will use this as the similarity measure in our work.

Let O_1 and O_2 be a pair of ontologies represented as labeled graphs, and O_{MMA} be the ontology induced by the similarity result S_{MMA} obtained by applying the basic MMA match algorithm (which combines the similarity measures in a single step/level operation). Let S_{strc} be the structural similarity measure S, calculated as follows, which defines the similarities between the concepts provided by O_{MMA} and those in the original ontologies O_1 and O_2.

$$S_{strc} = 2 \left|r(O_{MMA})\right| / (\left|r(O_{MMA}(O_1))\right| + \left|r(O_{MMA}(O_2))\right|) .$$

where $|r(O_{MMA})|$ is the number of relationships in ontology O_{MMA}, and $|r(O_{MMA}(O_i))|$ is the number of relationships in the immediate neighborhood of O_{MMA} in O_i. This neighborhood of O_{MMA} consists of the relationships of O_i with at least one end (one of the edge's end) belonging to O_{MMA}.

We view S_{strc} as a complementary measure to the output of MMA, applied in the second level. This is justified as follows.

- The structure similarity S_{strc} is mainly based on the presence of common concepts between the matched ontologies induced by the states calculated by MMA, and
- the similarity degree between the matched ontologies may still exist, even when there is no structural match in the result of MMA, i.e., when $S_{strc} = 0$.

Accordingly, the combined similarity measure S is relative to S_{MMA}, and should not be zero in case $S_{strc} = 0$. We further "smooth" the effect of S_{strc} as follws:

$$S = S_{MMA} + (x * S_{strc}), \quad where \quad x = (1 - S_{MMA}).$$

In the combined similarity S, suppose $S_{strc} = 0$. This then means S just depends on the similarity measure of MMA. On the other hand, if $S_{strc} = 1$, the neighborhood of the concepts matched by MMA is the same, and consequently S will take the maximum value, and since $1 = S_{MMA} + x$, we have that $x = 1 - S_{MMA}$, representing the complementary part of information described in the relationships among the concepts in a desired state found by MMA.

As we do not want to miss a matching state found which includes a large number of concepts matched, S_{MMA} provides possible good matches in the input ontologies together with the similarity degrees. The extended method will determine the same collection of matched states, but with better differentiation among them by taking into account the structural measures in the second level. An extension of this two level method to a multi-level method is straightforward, when the user can identify which measures could or should be applied at which level.

3 Structure-Based Multi Level Matching Algorithm

Now we study various matching spaces, and show how to construct the matching spaces. Then, we describe an algorithm to solve OMP, using MLMA.

3.1 The MLMA Algorithm

There are many algorithms for matching spaces. The notion of multispace "combines" all desired spaces into a single unified space. By searching from space to space, the matching algorithm can find a reasonable solution eventually. The main idea of the proposed Multi-Level algorithm is shown in Fig. 5.

The algorithm is mainly divided into three phases. In phase 1, which is the initialization phase, an initial assignment for the matching matrix *Map* is provided, as well as the functions of similarity to evaluate the relationship matrix. In phase 2 of MMA, which is the search phase, it is an iterative refinement for the *Map* matrices. In phase 3, the resulting mapping states from MMA will be qualified based on the connectivity among their concepts. Then, the best possible final state will be offered to the user.

The algorithm iteratively constructs matching spaces for entities of both S and T (see illustrative example in the next section). Then, the *Map* matrices will be evaluated according to the re/used spaces such as name and linguistic spaces, and finally the mapping state with the highest evaluation value will be offered to the user. If we only search one matching space, the algorithm behaves and computes as a single matcher; otherwise, it is indeed a multi-matcher. This design is useful as it provides a flexible and convenient way to use various relevant information about input ontologies, and to combine feasible mapping methods to obtain a far better matching result than the results obtained by each individual method. The method can employ any desired search algorithm.

```
Given: Two ontologies S and T
Output: The mapping result between S and T
Phase 1 Initialization
      Design an initial assignment matching matrix.
      /* For example, let Map be the zero matrix,
      or let diagonal elements in Map be equal to 1, and so
      on.*/
      Use the similarity functions to evaluate similarity or
      relationship matrix.
Phase 2 Search Matching Space
    begin
      Enter an active search space
      /* such as the name matching space */
      Evaluate an intermediate matching state
      /* more better matching results */
       begin
            Enter another active search space
            /* such as the linguistic matching space */
            Evaluate a better intermediate matching state
              Begin
                ...
                /* various available matching spaces,
              i.e. many feasible matching methods */
                  end;
         end;
         if the intermediate matching state is not
            the final solution
            /* the matching result does not satisfy
              the evaluation function */
            then use it as an initial solution in the
            next iteration;
              if the matching instance satisfies the
                 evaluation function
                 then return the final solution
      end;

Phase 3 Apply the Complementary measures
            /* Apply the structure similarity measure
              to the output of phase 2. */
```

Fig. 5. The Multi-Level Match Algorithm

3.2 Multiple Matching Spaces

Matching spaces are distinguished by diverse similarity measures. Moreover, the different kinds of similarity measures between the entities of the ontologies use different methods to compare the similarity of two ontologies. Accordingly, we construct the similarity matrices and matching spaces. Furthermore, different relation spaces are built on the result of using different methods of measuring similarity. These methods can be classified as follows (see [12] for more detailed explanation).

- *String similarity.* These methods are based on the hypothesis that concepts and property names representing semantic similarity will have similar syntactic features. The Levenshtein distance is the simplest implementation of string distance.
- *Linguistic similarity.* This is an extension of string similarity measures with some semantics. For example, considering the synonyms based on some specific thesauri, e.g., WordNet.

- *Structure-Aware*. This refers to approaches that take into account the structural layout of the ontologies considered, e.g., graph matching.
- *Context-Aware*. This is more semantically rich than structure similarity. In such method, a variety of relationships among concepts are considered in order to uniquely distinguish types of connections among the nodes in labeled directed graph matching.
- *Extension-Aware*. Classifications of the instances reflect the semantics of ontology. Data mining and Information Retrieval (IR) techniques are used to determine the hidden correspondence between instances.
- *Intension-Aware*. These techniques find correlations between relations among extent and intent, e.g., information flow.
- *Semantic similarity*. These focus more on logical correspondences, e.g., satisfiability.

4 Illustrative Scenario

In this scenario, we describe the main idea of the MLMA. Fig. 6. shows two sample taxonomies for Researchers (O_1) and Students (O_2) of different universities.

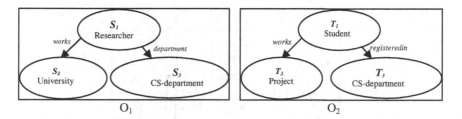

Fig. 6. Researchers (O_1) and Students (O_2) ontologies

We have to integrate the ontolgies into a single ontology. For reducing the manual work involved, we use a matching algorithm to identify the matching entities, and then help the middleware to integrate the schemas. For ease of presentation, we use very simple and small taxonomies.

As can be seen in Fig. 6, entities S_1, S_2, S_3, and T_1, T_2, T_3 are *concepts*, which are high-level entities in the input ontologies.

For ease of explanation, we only use two different similarity measures to compare the entities in S and T, name similarity (Levenshtein distance) and linguistic similarity (WordNet). We thus obtain the following similarity matrices for the *concepts*.

$$L_{name\_concept} = \begin{bmatrix} 0.0 & 0.2 & 0.308 \\ 0.2 & 0.2 & 0.0 \\ 0.308 & 0.308 & 1.0 \end{bmatrix}. \quad L_{ling\_concept} = \begin{bmatrix} 0.75 & 0.181 & 0.307 \\ 0.4 & 0.181 & 0.0 \\ 0.307 & 0.166 & 1.0 \end{bmatrix}.$$

This induces two similarity spaces: name space and linguistic space. When an assignment is found for matching space, we check the similarities of entities to see whether they exceed a user-defined threshold, denoted as *th*. The choice of the threshold value is application dependent and should be adjusted and suitably chosen for each space. The automation of selecting the suitable threshold value is left for future investigations. We define the following evaluation function, which measures the threshold value for the states obtained by the first phase of the MLMA algorithm.

$$v = \left(Map_{0-1} \cdot L\right)/k = \sum_{i=1}^{n} \sum_{j=1}^{m} Map_{0-1}(i, j).L(i, j) \bigg/ \sum_{i=1}^{n} \sum_{j=1}^{m} Map_{0-1}(i, j) \geq th \ .$$

where k is the number of matched pairs.

We now provide a brief description of the search process. The initial state of the mapping matrix is a zero matrix. Then, if the search process exceeds the maximum iteration, the maximum similarity states (Map_{max}) will be offered as the final mapping result. Also, we need to set the additive constraints in the search process. For this example, since the number of concepts in S is equal to that in T, we consider the ontologies S and T have been fully matched. So, the mapping states of concepts include 6 entries now, e_1, e_2, ..., e_6 as shown in Fig. 7.

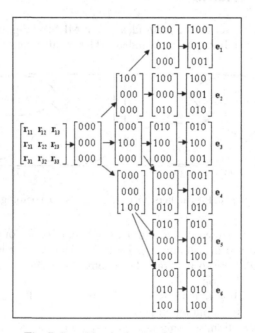

Fig. 7. Searching in the matching space

The outputs of MMA are states e_1, e_2, ..., e_6 shown in Fig. 8, which are represented as labeled directed graphs, in general.

As shown in Table 1, e_1 indicates the "best" matching found. Using the formula for computing the threshold values for name and linguistic similarity matrices $L_{name\_concept}$ and $L_{ling\_concept}$ above, we get values 0.4 and 0.64 for name similarity v_1 and linguistic similarity v_2, respectively.

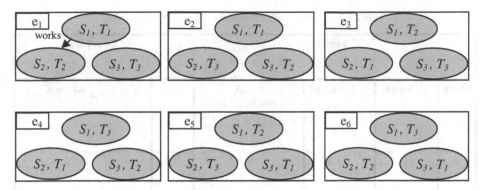

Fig. 8. The states determined by MMA

To measure S_{strc} for the mapping state e_1:

- The number of common relationships between the common concepts that connect these concepts to other common concepts is equal 1.
- The number of relationships in O_1 with at least one end belonging to the common concepts is equal 2.
- The number of relationships in O_2 with at least one end belonging to the common concepts is equal 2.

As a result, we obtain $S_{strc} = ((2*1)/(2+2))=0.5$.

Table 1 shows the individual and combined similarity match results for each state e_i. Note that if we only use the name similarity space, the mapping result would be e_3. In the same way, if we only use the linguistic space, we would obtain e_1 as the result. Also, using $Map_{name\_concept}$, $Map_{ling\_concept}$, and the threshold value *th* we obtain S_{MMA}. Consequently, the output result state e_1 means that we matched n concepts from the source ontology S to the m concepts from the target ontology T. That is, s_1 matched with t_1, s_2 with t_2, and s_3 with t_3. Accordingly, the algorithm matches the properties and/or instances of each matched pairs of the concepts. One could also build a logic based space using, say description logics [3], and employ reasoning techniques to decide subsumption between two concepts.

We can also notice the recognized performance of the measure and how the S_{MMA} and S_{strc} similarities are combined to compute the final measure S. The scenario indicates that S is always grater than or equal S_{MMA} for our similarity measures. This leads to the fact that S increases the weight of those states with connected common concepts than the states of common concepts that are not connected.

As a result, using S we gain the following:

- S maintains as many as possible number of matched concepts
- S can improve the performance of S_{MMA}, if the ontologies that are to be matched are structurally similar. However, it will not affect S_{MMA} even if there is no structure similarity at all in the given input ontologies.

Table 1. Individual and combined similarity match results

		Level 1			Level 2
State	Name v_1	Concept v_2	S_{MMA} Normalized cost $v = (v_1 + v_2)/2$	S_{strc}	$S = S_{MMA} + (x * S_{strc})$
e_1	0.4	**0.64**	**0.52**	0.5	**0.77**
e_2	0.103	0.305	0.204	0.0	0.204
e_3	**0.466**	0.527	0.497	0.0	0.497
e_4	0.272	0.291	0.282	0.0	0.282
e_5	0.169	0.163	0.166	0.0	0.166
e_6	0.269	0.265	0.267	0.0	0.267

5 Experimentation and Results

In our evaluation we have used three pairs of ontologies as benchmarks: (1) the MIT bibtex ontology[1] (contains 43 named classes, 22 object properties, 24 data properties) and the UMBC publication ontology[2] (contains 15 named classes, 5 object properties, 27 data properties) which are publicly available, (2) computer ontologies (the first onltology contains 17 named classes, 11 object properties, 15 data properties, and the second one contains 15 named classes, 10 object properties, and 14 data properties), and (3) ontologies about computer science departments; the first onltology contains 16 named classes, 12 object properties, 10 data properties, and the second one contains 18 named classes, 14 object properties, and 9 data properties. We have created the second and third pairs of the ontologies.

As match quality measures, we have used the following indicators: *precision, recall, and F-measure. Precision* is a value in the [0, 1] range; the higher the value, the smaller is the set of wrong mappings (false positives) computed. *Recall* varies in the [0,1] range; the higher this value, the smaller is the set of correct mappings (true positives) not found. *F-measure* varies in the [0,1] range, which is a global measure of the matching quality. The version computed here is the harmonic mean of precision and recall [6].

---

[1] http://visus.mit.edu/bibtex/0.1/bibtex.owl
[2] http://ebiquity.umbc.edu/ontology/publication.owl

In a testing methodology, we are concerned with providing a ground for evaluating the quality of match results. For this, we have determined expert matches for all the input pairs of ontologies. The results produced by the matcher have been compared with these expert mappings.

The evaluation results are shown in Fig. 9. From the point of view of the quality of the matching results, the proposed MLMA method clearly outperforms the other techniques.

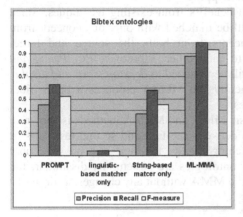

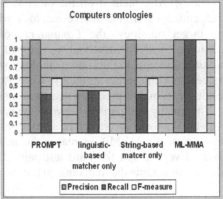

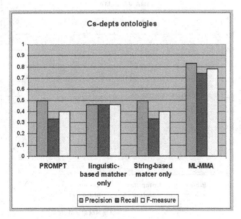

Fig. 9. Experimentation and Results

The key point in MLMA is that it gives for each entity from the source ontology only one corresponding entity match from the target ontology. This enables MLMA to achieve in these cases high precession and recall numbers. For instance, in the case of the computers ontologies, since both ontologies contain either the same names for the corresponding entities, or they use totally different names, we see that the string-based techniques provided a high precision rates (no wrong mappings returned to the user), that is, the concept *'Computers'* in the source ontology is mapped to the *'Computers'* concept in the target ontology. However, the string-based techniques reported a low recall rate because they failed to identify semantic mappings. For example, the string-based technique missed to match the concepts (*PC, Price, and Monitor*) in the source ontology to their corresponding concepts (*desktop, cost, and display*) in the target ontology.

The semantics-based techniques had low precision rates (some even returned incorrect mappings to the user). For instance, the concept Computers in the source ontology will also be matched with the desktop and laptop concepts in the target ontology. Also, the reason for the low recall rate is that it gives a large set of wrong mappings compared with the expert defined mappings.

The MLMA method on the other hand benefits from existing techniques. Since each concept from the source ontology will be matched with only one concept from the target ontology, the *Computers* concepts from both, the source and target ontologies will be identified as mapped to each other. Moreover, *PC, Price, and Monitor* concepts in the source ontology will be matched to *desktop, cost, and display* concepts in the target ontology. Consequently the MLMA produces a better final result for its higher precision and recall rates.

The quality comparison between the basic MMA and MLMA methods is shown in Fig. 10. As there are structure similarities between the first and second test pairs of ontologies, the MLMA increases the matching quality for their best possible final states. Even though the third test pairs of ontologies are structurally dissimilar, the MLMA maintains the matching quality of the MMA without any changes, as desired.

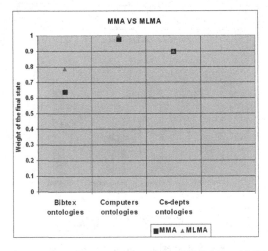

Fig. 10. The quality comparison between the basic MMA and MLMA methods

6 Related Work

The RiMOM system [14] integrates multiple strategies such as, edit distance, statistical learning, and three similarity propagation based strategies. Then, RiMOM applies a strategy selection method in order to decide which strategy will rely more on it. As a result, RiMOM combines the conducted alignment using linear interpolation method. Similarity Flooding [17] and AnchorPrompt [20] compare graphs representing ontologies, and look for similarities in the graph structures. GLUE [4] employs machine-learning techniques to find mappings. It uses multiple learners and exploits information in concept instances and taxonomy structures of ontologies. GLUE uses a probabilistic model to combine results of different learners. The notion of similarity it uses is based on k-statistics which can be thought of as being defined over the joint probability of the concepts involved. The work proposed in [18] describes an ontology match enhance tool that improves existing ontology matching algorithms based on probabilistic inferences.

The algorithm in [8] uses a complete proof procedure to decide subsumption or equivalence between classes, given initial equivalence of some classes and analysis of the relationships in the taxonomy. The work in [16] has a matching engine which contains diverse libraries that supports many match algorithms and strategies. In [16] they combine the match results by aggregating the results of the applied matchers on the given input ontologies. Then the selected result will be made using e.g. threshold value. In addition, a number of other systems use machine learning techniques for finding class similarity from instances [5]. Falcon-AO [11] has three elementary matchers; Linguistics matchers (V-DOC and I-sub) and structural matcher (GMO). The results of falcon-AO mainly derived either from the alignments generated from linguistic or structural matchers based on which has a higher results. Otherwise, the Falcon-AO results will be generated by making a combination among both linguistic and structural matchers with a weighting scheme. Some researchers propose similarity metrics between concepts in different ontologies based on their relationships to other concepts. For example, a similarity metric between concepts in OWL ontologies [7] is a weighted combination of similarities of various features in OWL concept definitions including their labels, domains and ranges of properties, restrictions on properties (such as cardinality restrictions), types of concepts, subclasses and super classes, and so on. Algorithms such as in [10] make use of derived graphs or alternative representations such as the pair wise connectivity graphs.

There are two features which make our approach distinct from the aforementioned algorithms and systems. The first point is the way how the similarities are transformed into mappings is measured using a space search technique in order to deal with a many to many match problem. The second point is, in contrast to other approaches such as [10] our proposed similarity measure ensures that our approach works even in the case if there are no structure similarities in the given input ontologies.

7 Conclusions and Future Work

We proposed a new method for ontology matching that uses Multi-space search techniques together with a flexible measure that is based on well-known graph algorithm to obtain the best possible matching results. A main characteristic of our technique is that it combines existing matching techniques to provide a solution to a given ontology matching problem. Moreover, the optimal matching state has been considered based on its rich structure on one hand, and the number of common concepts of the matched ontologies on other hand. As a result, applying our mapping transformation and similarity measure methods will not decrease the number of matching concepts (*size*), and will increase the similarity measure of the state that has high structural similarity among its concepts (*structure*). We have developed running prototypes of both the basic MMA and the proposed MLMA, and conducted experiments using some benchmark ontologies. Our results indicated that the proposed MLMA technique provided improved match results. As a future work, we would like to identify optimization opportunities in our context, and study the scalability (quantity) using larger ontologies.

Acknowledgements. This work was supported in part by grants from Natural Sciences and Engineering Research Council (NSERC) of Canada, and by Libyan Ministry of Education.

References

1. Alasoud, A., Haarslev, V., Shiri, N.: A hybrid approach for ontology integration. In: Proc. VLDB Workshop on Ontologies-based techniques for DataBases and Information Systems (ODBIS), Trondheim, Norway, September 2-3, 2005 (2005)
2. Artale, A., Franconi, E., Mandreoli, F.: Description logics for modeling dynamic information. In: Logics for Emerging Applications of Databases. Springer, Heidelberg (2003)
3. Baader, F., Celanese, D., McGuinness, D., Nardi, D., Patel-Schneider, P.: The Description Logic Handbook: Theory, Implementation, and Applications. Cambridge University Press, Cambridge (2003)
4. Doan, A., Madhavan, J., Domingos, P., Halevy, A.: Learning to map between ontologies on the semantic web. In: Proc. 11th Int'l WWW Conference, Hawaii, US (2002)
5. Doan, A., Madhavan, J., Domingos, P., Halevy, A.: Ontology matching: A machine learning approach. In: Staab, S., Studer, R. (eds.) Handbook on Ontologies in Information Systems, pp. 397–416. Springer, Berlin (2003)
6. Do, H.H., Melnik, S., Rahm, E.: Comparison of schema matching evaluations. In: Proc. workshop on Web and Databases (2002)
7. Euzenat, J., Valtchev, P.: Similarity-based ontology alignment in OWL-Lite. In: Proc. 16th European Conference on Artificial Intelligence (ECAI-04), Valencia, Spain (2004)
8. Giunchiglia, F., Shvaiko, P.: Semantic matching. In: Proc. IJCAI Workshop on ontologies and distributed systems, pp. 139–146 (2003)
9. Gu, J.: Multispace search for satisfiability and NP-hard problems. DIMACS Series in Discrete Mathematics and Theoretical Computer Science 35, 407–517 (1997)
10. Hu, W., Jian, N.S., Qu, Y.Z., Wang, Y.B.: GMO: A Graph Matching for Ontologies. In: Proc. K-Cap Workshop on Integrating Ontologies, pp. 43–50 (2005)
11. Hu, W., Cheng, G., Zheng, D., Zhong, X., Qu, Y.: The results of Falcon-AO. In: Proc. International workshop on Ontology Matching (OM), Athens, Georgia, U.S.A, November 5, 2006 (2006)
12. Kalfoglou, Y., Hu, B.: CROSI Mapping System (CMS). In: Proc. Integrating Ontologies Workshop, Banff, Canada, October 2, 2005 (2005)
13. Li, W., Clifton, C.: SEMINT: A tool for identifying attribute correspondences in heterogeneous databases using neural networks. IEEE Trans. on Data & Knowledge Engineering 33(1), 49–84 (2000)

14. Li, Y., Li, J., Zhang, D., Tang, J.: Results of ontology alignment with RiMOM. In: Proc. International workshop on Ontology Matching (OM), Athens, Georgia, U.S.A, November 5, 2006 (2006)
15. Madhavan, J., Bernstein, P.A., Rahm, E.: Generic schema matching with cupid. In: Proc. 27th VLDB Conference (2001)
16. Massmann, S., Engmann, D., Rahm, E., Tang, J.: Results of ontology alignment with COMA++. In: Proc. International workshop on Ontology Matching (OM), Athens, Georgia, U.S.A, November 5, 2006 (2006)
17. Melnik, S., Garcia-Molina, H., Rahm, E.: Similarity flooding: A versatile graph matching algorithm and its application to schema matching. In: 18th Int. Conference on Data Engineering (ICDE), San Jose, California (2002)
18. Mitra, P., Noy, N.F., Jaiswal, A.R.: OMEN: A probabilistic ontology mapping tool. In: Proc. Workshop on Meaning Coordination and Negotiation, Hisroshima, Japan (2004)
19. Noy, N.F., Musen, M.A.: The PROMPT suite: Interactive tools for ontology merging and mapping. Journal of Human-Computer Studies 59(6), 983–1024 (2003)
20. Noy, N.F., Musen, M.A.: Anchor-PROMPT: Using non-local context for semantic matching. In: Proc. Workshop on Ontologies and Information Sharing (in conjunction with IJCAI), Seattle, WA (2001)
21. Rasmussen, E.: Clustering Algorithms. In: Frakes, W.B., Baeza–Yates, R. (eds.) Information Retrieval: Data Structures & Algorithms, Prentice Hall, Englewood Cliffs (1992)
22. Zhang, Z., Che, H.Y., Shi, P.F., Sun, Y., Gu, J.: An algebraic framework for schema matching. In: Fan, W., Wu, Z., Yang, J. (eds.) WAIM 2005. LNCS, vol. 3739, Springer, Heidelberg (2005)

Class Structures and Lexical Similarities of Class Names for Ontology Matching

Sumit Sen[1,2], Suman Somavarapu[1], and N.L. Sarda[1]

[1] Deptt of Computer Science, IIT Bombay, Mumbai-76 India
[2] IfGI, University of Münster, Robert-Koch Str. 26, 48149 Münster, Germany
sumitsen@uni-muenster.de, {suman,nls}@cse.iitb.ac.in

Abstract. Semantic Interoperability is a major issue for National Spatial data Infrastructures (NSDIs) and mapping across heterogeneous databases is essential for such interoperability. Mapping of schemas based on ontology mapping provides opportunities for semantic translation of schemas elements and hence for database queries across heterogeneous sources. Such semantics based mappings are usually human centered processes. This paper demonstrates semi-automatic mapping using semantic similarity values from an electronic lexicon. Lexical similarity of class names and class structures constitute knowledge base for mapping between two schemas. We employ semantic mapping based on synonym similarity matches from WordNet. We use heuristics based propagation of similarities using attribute mapping and superclass-subclass relations. The machine based similarity values are seen to be comparable to human generated values of mapping.

Keywords: ontology, semantic mapping, lexical similarity, similarity propagation, heterogeneous databases.

1 Introduction

Spatial databases usually store information relating to different themes but also spatial information of the records. The spatial information, serves as the common geospatial domain for such databases serves as a central point of integrated usage of such data. Geographic Information Systems and more recently, Web Mapping Services (WMS) as promulgated by the Open Geospatial Consortium (OGC) [1], display geospatial data from such spatial databases. With increased possibilities of sharing of databases across domains and user groups based on frameworks such as geospatial web services and Spatial Data Infrastructures (SDIs), the need for resolving the semantic interoperability of data has been identified as a major requirement. National Spatial Data Infrastructures (NSDIs) can be considered as a typical testbed for semantic interoperability experiments across heterogeneous database users.

Semantic mapping across heterogeneous data sources is reported as a major requirement for National Spatial Data Infrastructures [2]. Such Infrastructures serve as a common interaction mechanism between multiple organizations which need to share geospatial data for their different applications. Figure 2 shows a typical scenario

M. Collard (Ed.): ODBIS 2005/2006, LNCS 4623, pp. 18–36, 2007.

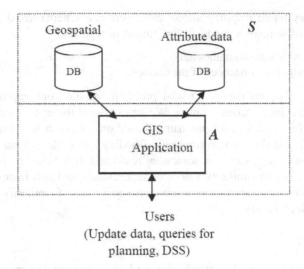

Fig. 1. Geospatial data usage scenario in an NSDI. The two types of data sources include geospatial data sources and attribute data sources. The semantics of the data source region S need not be same as that of the application region A.

of data sharing in an NSDI with multiple (semantically heterogeneous) data sources being used. The traditional view of interoperability in an NSDI is based on mapping of information sources based on human based interaction and documentation. A strictly *Top-Down* approach advocating use of fixed class names can be seen as too rigid and impractical for actual use. On the other hand, schema mappings based on a bottom-up approach is difficult even if mappings can be achieved by organizations participating in the NSDI because

(1) Schemas are continuously evolving
(2) Human knowledge about semantics of the table names and attribute names are often not completely expressed in the names used. Therefore mapping should be seen as a probability based process.
(3) It is not necessary that mappings exists always. In a probability based model this situation is equated with zero values. On the other hand it is not possible or necessary to have values for every mapping. Such cases where the mapping is not done should be equated to null values of probability of mapping.

In addition to these observations about schema mappings of databases in an NSDI we also observe that organizations can join or leave the Infrastructure. Depending on this, new mappings need to be generated at times and older mappings need to evolve.

It is imperative that a semi-automatic process of mapping of databases need to evolve. Ontology based mapping has been increasingly viewed as an engineering solution to the problems. Based on specifications of the conceptualizations [3] as a more generic layer above the schema specifications, ontologies serve as an intermediate step to specify and resolve semantics of the contents of a database system. Ontology based mapping allows us to generate schema translation rules [4]. Two categories of semantics can be differentiated in regard to

(a) Classes or schema names and
(b) Individuals or instances of the classes.

While the later is by no means a trivial problem we state our approach based on semantics of the class or schema names. We aim to assist the generation of semantics based mapping for classes or schema names based on lexicon based similarity values. The approach is similar to the similarity flooding principle [5] but in our case, propagation of similarity values is somewhat restricted. It is based on heuristics such that class attributes and similarity values of superclasses and subclasses are reflected in the overall similarity values. The machine based values of similarity are compared to human generated values.

1.1 Paper Outline

This section has provided the introduction and also explains the motivation of this work. § 2 outlines the previous work in semantic mapping generation and describes the research problem at hand. Subsequently § 3 describes the generation of lexical similarity values and their propagation based on attribute properties of classes and their superclass -subclass structures.[1] In § 4 we analyze the similarity values vis-à-vis human generated values. We also provide the outline of a mechanism to translate data from different sources based on the ontology mapping with a target domain in § 5. Some conclusions and areas for future work are identified in the end.

1.2 Motivation

The motivation of our research is derived from efforts to achieve schema translations from heterogeneous databases that participate in the NSDI. Since the objective of sharing of resources in the NSDI is to maximize the usage of data and applications, the requirement of allowing semantics based translations of queries and data is primary in nature. We restrict our problems based on logical steps as follows:

(i)   To identify the translations (in the form of XQuery statements), which could be applied to interface semantically heterogeneous systems in the NSDI
(ii)   To generate such translations based on mappings between the ontologies of the two systems
(iii) To semi-automate the process of mapping between the ontologies

The last step is rather the focus of this paper. Such Mapping between ontologies is dependent on both the explicit semantics of the class names or attribute names and also the implicit semantics of subclasses and superclass relations. When we consider the objective of translations it is important to have a directional mapping such that all members of the target schema mapped to the source schema as shown in figure 2.

---

[1] The term *Class Structure* in this paper refers to three different constituents -the attributes of the class, its superclasses and subclasses.

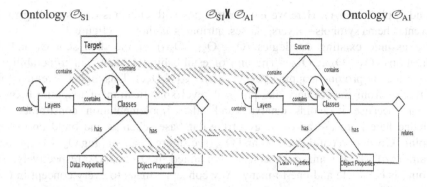

Fig. 2. Ontology mapping between Target and Source. The different components of the Source ontology including layers, classes and their properties are mapped to each other. Layers can be considered as a group of classes. Classes can have inherited classes and so can layers. The relation between of layers and classes is not that of inheritance but rather that of aggregation.

2   Generating Semantic Mapping

Semantic Mapping can be considered as process, which generates rules for transformations between different data sources which do not necessarily have the same semantics for the same schema symbols. Schema symbols[2], for our case consists of layer names, class names and property names. We also need to be clear that having different semantics for the same schema symbols also entails that sometimes

1   Same symbols could have different meanings
2   Different symbols could have the same meaning
3   Some symbols in the first schema may not have corresponding symbols with the same meanings in second schema
4   Some symbols in the first schema could correspond to more than one symbol in the second schema such that the meaning is conveyed by simple aggregation (or further complex functions of aggregation) of the multiple symbols in the second schema
5   Some symbols in the first schema could correspond to part of a symbol in the second schema such that the meaning can be extracted fully from that corresponding symbol.
6   Also some symbols in the first schema could correspond to multiple symbols in the second schema but combining aspect 4 and 5 above.

Besides these we know that datatype heterogeneities (different datatype for the same schema component in different databases) are closely associated to the above contexts but we shall assume their absence for our case.

As discussed in the introduction, we use ontology based mapping to achieve schema translations. Now consider the situation described in figure 1 with attribute data source

---

[2] We refer to schema elements as schema symbols to stress that these symbols have certain meaning and conceptualizations.

(S) and application (A). Here we have ontologies with elements corresponding to the different schema symbols – layers, classes, attributes as shown in figure 2.

We assume existing ontologies (O_{S1}, O_{S2}...O_{SM}) of the data sources and the applications (O_{A1}, O_{A2}...O_{AN}). The aim of establishing semantic interoperability is now reduced to provide mapping ($O_{S1}X$ O_{A1}...$O_{SM}X$ O_{SN}). This higher level mapping is different from the XQuery-like physical level specification of mapping between schemas because it avoids datatype and other implementation constraints. The challenge here is to use an ontology of the database schemas and build up explicit mapping. Given two ontologies O_{S1} and O_{A1} (see figure 2) a mapping $O_{S1}X$ O_{A1} is a set of pairs (s,a) where s and a are concept contained in O_{S1} and O_{A1} respectively. The mapping is complete and one-to-many. Any concept s maps to every concept in O_{A1w} but with different intensities which is dependent on how similar it is to the target concept. When such similarities are taken into consideration while determining the matching we can assume the highest mapping value as 1 and lowest as 0. Thus a mapping is defined as a matrix of similarity values as below

$$M[O_S X\ O_A] = \{m_{S1A1},\ m_{S1A2},..\ m_{S1An}$$
$$m_{S2A1},\ m_{S2A2},...\ m_{S2An} \tag{1}$$
$$......$$
$$m_{Sm,A1},\ m_{SmA2},...\ m_{SmAn}\}$$

such that $0 \le m_{XY} \le 1$

The values of semantic similarity are dependent on the notion of semantics which is employed. The similarity matrix can be used across ontologies if the notion of semantics is consistent.

We discuss the previous work in the area of computing similarities for schema matching in the next section. Thereafter we explain the theoretical basis of our research problem.

2.1 Previous Work

Similarity based approach for schema mapping has been studied using different approaches. Shvaiko [6] has classified schema matching approaches and has discussed the heuristics based approaches both at structure and element level. The Similarity Flooding approach [5] as implemented in Rondo [8] utilizes a hybrid-matching algorithm based on the ideas of similarity propagation. Schemas are presented as directed labeled graphs; the algorithm manipulates them in an iterative fix-point computation to produce mapping between the nodes of the input graphs. The technique starts from string-based comparison (common prefixes, suffixes tests) of the vertices' labels to obtain an initial mapping which is refined within the fix-point computation. The basic concept behind the SF algorithm is the similarity spreading from similar nodes to the adjacent neighbors through propagation coefficients. From iteration to iteration the spreading depth and a similarity measure are increasing till the fix-point is reached. The result of this step is a refined mapping which is further filtered to finalize the matching process.

Cupid [9] implements a hybrid matching algorithm comprising linguistic and structural schema matching techniques, and computes similarity coefficients with the assistance of a precompiled thesaurus. Input schemas are encoded as graphs. Nodes represent schema elements and are traversed in a combined bottom-up and top-down manner. Matching algorithm consists of three phases and operates only with tree-structures to which no-tree cases are reduced. The first phase (linguistic matching) computes linguistic similarity coefficients between schema element names (labels) based on morphological normalization, categorization, string-based techniques (common prefixes, suffixes tests) and a thesaurus look-up. The second phase (structural matching) computes structural similarity coefficients weighted by leaves which measure the similarity between contexts in which individual schema elements occur. The third phase (mapping generation) computes weighted similarity coefficients and generates final mappings by choosing pairs of schema elements with weighted similarity coefficients, which are higher than a given threshold. Both Rondo [8] and Cupid [9] are important to our approach because they allow propagation of semantic similarity, which is important to integrate the explicit and implicit semantic matching definitions stated previously. For a complete survey of other schema matching approaches see [6] and [10].

Lexical matching in ontologies has also been studied in detail in Semantic integration approaches using ontologies. A survey by Noy [10] separates matching approaches based on

   (i) shared upper ontologies based approaches and
   (ii) heuristics based machine learning approaches

While both of the above are said to have advantages in different objective settings, the later is significant in the absence of a commitment to a shared upper ontology. The mappings in this case need to be stored as GAV or LAV similar to the approach in schema matching based on directional mappings [11] and with an overall objective of allowing query answering across heterogeneous data. The Heuristics based approaches are reported to employ automatic or semi-automatic techniques by looking at

- concept names
- class hierarchies
- property definitions
- instance definitions class descriptions (as Description Logic statements)

While instance based approaches such as GLUE [12] can be seen as helpful to understand the ontology commitment of the instances, the luxury of availability of time and access to the data instances cannot be assumed. Giunchiglia and Shvaiko [13] on the other hand use WordNet as a common source for grounding. Subsequently mappings such as generalizations, specializations, and disjointness are determined using a SAT prover.

2.2 The Ontology Mapping Problem

An assessment of the problems of semantic interoperability in spatial data infrastructures can be seen in [14] Semantic mapping is reported to work at two levels-(1) explicit semantics of the schema elements and (2) implicit semantics resulting from schema structure including class hierarchies and attribute properties. We divide these based on the following definitions

Definition 1. A mapping M is defined to be reflective of *explicit semantics of the schema* elements if and only if every schema element that maps to another schema element, can substitute the later in the absence of any schema structure.

In a lexicon such substitution entails that one is a synonym of the other.

Example 1: For a mapping M [A, B] = {1, 0, 0, 1} where A={road, intersection} B = {street, crossing} we can say that it reflects explicit semantics of A and B if one could substitute 'road' by 'street' and 'crossing' by 'intersection'. In WordNet [7] this condition would be true. Also if this criterion can be proved, the mapping can be termed as reflective of explicit semantics of the schema elements.

Definition 2. A mapping M is defined to be reflective of *implicit semantics resulting from super-class structures* if and only if every element that maps to another element in the structure, has similar super classes and attributes (Also the related super classes have the same criteria with respect to its own super-classes and attributes)

Example 2: For a mapping M[A, B] = {1, 0, 0, 1} where A and B have two elements each, let us assume one element of both A and B are sub classes of the other and represented in figure 3. Here only if the explicit similarity of attributes of element1 of A and element1 of B are higher M is reflective of implicit semantics of the super class structure. In this case the explicit similarity of attributes of Element 1 of A and Element 2 of B should be 0 and so also that of attributes of element 2 of A and element1 of B. In regard to the implicit semantics of super-class we can say that since element 2 of both A and B have similar super-classes, their own similarity value is

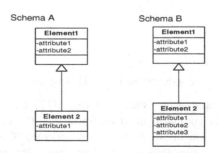

Fig. 3. Implicit semantics of the super class structure

higher than the original implicit value of similarity and explicit similarity of the attributes combined.

Definition 3. A mapping M is defined to be reflective of *implicit semantics resulting from sub-class structures* if and only if every element that maps to another element in the structure, has similar sub classes and attributes. Also the related sub classes have the same criteria with respect to its own sub-classes and attributes.

Example 3: For a mapping M[A, B] = { 1, 0, 0, 1} where A and B have two elements each, let us assume one element of both A and B are sub classes of the other and represented in figure 4. The relation to similarity of attributes of Element1 and Element2 in both A and B is the same as explained in Example 2. In regard to the implicit semantics of sub-class we can say that since element 1 of both A and B have similar sub-classes, their own similarity value is higher than the original implicit value of similarity and explicit similarity of the attributes combined. (Note that here subclasses have same number of attributes although the significance of equal number of attributes cannot be considered as critical as is the case in Example 2)

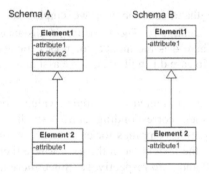

Fig. 4. Implicit semantics of the sub class structure

Definition 4. A mapping M is defined to be reflective of *complete semantics resulting from both schema structure and semantics of elements* if and only if the mapping is reflective of implicit semantics of attributes, super-class and sub-class structures and explicit semantics of schema elements.

Let us be clear that definition 1 does not qualify as a syntactic match of the labels of the schema elements. The substitutability sense implied here involves semantics and implied meaning of the label. This may not be clear from the label name alone and usually requires a more verbose description. Secondly since definition 4 can be seen as a combination of the other three definitions, we define our problem stepwise: to obtain mappings which are reflective of

   a. Explicit semantics of the schema elements
   b. Implicit semantics of the super-class schema structure
   c. Implicit semantics of the sub-class schema structure

3 Semantic Mapping Generation

We describe the approach of generating the semantic mapping as a three step process, namely (i) generating values of lexical similarity based on synonym relations (ii) propagating the similarity values for sub classes and similarly for superclasses (iii) combining the values of step (ii) to obtain the most similar classes and attributes (of the source ontology) for each class and attribute of the target ontology. We describe each step as below.

3.1 Generating Lexical Similarity Values

Definition 5. Lexical similarity S is a function defined between two element names x and y where

$$S(x,y)= \beta(\text{measure of the distance of the two words in a lexicon})$$

Such that $0 \leq S(x, y) \leq 1$

Remark 1. β is a weigthage function that we employ to sensitize our similarity function for optimality conditions. The measure of distance on the other hand is computed as the $(d)^{-4}$ where d is the number of nodes traversed in the graph of the lexicon (say WordNet). In case d is null or zero we assign a zero value to the measure of distance.

Lexical similarities are computed as binary values between two schemas components based on their corresponding entries in the lexicon. We assume a GAV approach by computing mappings for each target ontology. In the absence of a corresponding entry in the lexicon or in the case where there is no lexical relation we assume that d is null and zero respectively. Since there are two types of lexical relations in which we are interested (out of the 9 discussed by Evens and Smith [15]) we have lexical match algorithms for synonyms, hypernyms, and hyponym. For synonym relations the distance between two words is either 0 or 1 depending on their occurrence in a WordNet synset. For our case study the target ontology is that of Ordnance Survey UK [16] and source is OGC transportation schema (full version) [1]. We list lexical similarities of class names based on synonyms in column 3 of table 1 below.

3.2 Propagation of Similarities of Attributes and Superclasses

If attributes of the target class have high similarity values with respect to certain attributes of the source class, such a mapping stands to be more attractive in comparison to any mapping where the attributes do not yield high similarity values. This is based on the definition of implicit semantics of superclass relations of definition 2 we can obtain a no penalty algorithm for computing the propagated similarity value as shown below.

For all attributes
        Obtain lexical similarity matrix $M_a[O_S X\ O_T]$ for all attributes
End For
For all classes **do**
    Obtain lexical similarity matrix $M_c[O_S X\ O_T]$ such that class c_{T_q} in O_T has similarity
    value cm_{SpTq} with respect to class c_{Sp} in source ontology O_S

        For all attributes (a1, a2,...an) of c_{T_q} **do**

$$\text{If } \frac{\alpha(cm_{SpTq}) + \beta(a_{n\,SpTq})}{\alpha + \beta} > (cm_{SpTq}) \text{ then}$$

$$(cm_{SpTq}) = \frac{\alpha(cm_{SpTq}) + \beta(a_{n\,SpTq})}{\alpha + \beta}$$

        End If
        End For
End For

Set {ParentClassBasket} = Null

While {ParentClassBasket} < O_T
    For all Classes in O_T such that Parent Class p_{T_q} is in {ParentClassBasket}

$$\text{If } \frac{\varphi(cm_{SpTq}) + \phi(pm_{SpTq})}{\varphi + \phi} > (cm_{SpTq}) \text{ then}$$

$$(cm_{SpTq}) = \frac{\varphi(cm_{SpTq}) + \phi(pm_{SpTq})}{\varphi + \phi}$$

    End If
    Include c_{T_q} as member of {ParentClassBasket}
    End For
End While

Fig. 5. Algorithm for Propagation of similarity values of attributes and superclasses. $\alpha, \beta, \varphi, \phi,$ represent weightages of propagation.

In short this algorithm allows an increase of the similarity values if the combined value of similarity based on attribute similarity and thereafter, the superclass similarity has increased. The use of such weightages clearly shows the use of heuristics based measures. Table 1 below shows some values of improved similarity values using the propagation described above.

3.3 Propagation of Similarities of Attributes and Subclasses

The propagation in this case is similar but uses subclass similarity values instead of the superclass similarity values. Results of the propagation are shown in the table 2 below.

Table 1. Top class matches based on propagated values of similarity of supper classes and attributes

Target Class (c_{Tq})	Source Class (c_{Sp})	Lexical Similarity S(x,y)	Propagated Similarity (cm_{SpTq})
OS:RoadRouteInformation	OGC:RailRoadRoute	0,6666667	0,766666667
OS:InformationPoint	OGC:TransportationPoint	0,6052632	0,723684211
OS:InformationPoint	OGC:TransportationPoint	0,6052632	0,723684211
OS:RoadPartiaRouteInformation	OGC:RailRoadRoute	0,5714286	0,7
OS:road	OGC:RailRoadPoint	0,5	0,65
OS:road	OGC:RailRoadSegment	0,5	0,65
OS:road	OGC:RailRoadSwitch	0,5	0,65
OS:InformationPoint	OGC:TransportationPath	0,4166667	0,591666667
OS:InformationPoint	OGC:TransportationPath	0,4166667	0,591666667
OS:roadInformationMember	OGC:TransportationSegment	0,4047619	0,583333333
OS:roadLink	OGC:RailRoadStation	0,4	0,58
OS:roadLink	OGC:RailRoadPoint	0,4	0,58
OS:roadLink	OGC:RailRoadSegment	0,4	0,58
OS:roadLink	OGC:RailRoadRoute	0,4	0,58
OS:roadNode	OGC:RailRoadStation	0,4	0,58
OS:roadNode	OGC:RailRoadSegment	0,4	0,58
OS:roadNode	OGC:RailRoadRoute	0,4	0,58
OS:roadNode	OGC:RailRoadBridge	0,4	0,58

Table 2. Top class matches based on propagated values of similarity of subclasses and attributes

Target Class (c_{Tq})	Source Class (c_{Sp})	Lexical Similarity S(x,y)	Propagated Similarity (cm_{SpTq})
OS:RoadRouteInformation	OGC:RailRoadRoute	0,6666667	0,766666667
OS:InformationPoint	OGC:TransportationPoint	0,6052632	0,723684211
OS:RoadPartiaRouteInformation	OGC:RailRoadRoute	0,5714286	0,7
OS:road	OGC:RailRoadPoint	0,5	0,65
OS:road	OGC:RailRoadSegment	0,5	0,65
OS:road	OGC:RailRoadSwitch	0,5	0,65
OS:road	OGC:RailRoadStation	0,5	0,55000001
OS:road	OGC:RailRoadRoute	0,5	0,55000001
OS:road	OGC:RailRoadSignal	0,5	0,53
OS:road	OGC:RailRoadBridge	0,5	0,5
OS:InformationPoint	OGC:TransportationPath	0,4166667	0,591666667

Table 2. (*continued*)

OS:roadInformationMember	OGC:TransportationSegment	0,4047619	0,583333333
OS:roadLink	OGC:RailRoadStation	0,4	0,58
OS:roadLink	OGC:RailRoadPoint	0,4	0,58
OS:roadLink	OGC:RailRoadSegment	0,4	0,58

3.4 Most Similar Mappings

Generation of most similar mappings is based on a simple combination of the values generated from 3.2 and 3.3. We use weightages (50:50 and 70:30) to obtain two sets of most similar mappings. The basic lexical similarity values of both these mappings and also the attribute similarity propagation is same. The results are shown in the table 3 below.

Table 3. Top class matches based on overall similarity

Target Class	Source Class	Overall Similarity
(c_{Tq})	(c_{Sp})	(cm_{SpTq})
OS:InformationPoint	OGC:TransportationPath	0,591666667
OS:InformationPoint	OGC:TransportationPoint	0,723684211
OS:road	OGC:RailRoadPoint	0,65
OS:road	OGC:RailRoadSegment	0,65
OS:road	OGC:RailRoadSwitch	0,65
OS:roadInformationMember	OGC:TransportationSegment	0,583333333
OS:roadLink	OGC:RailRoadPoint	0,58
OS:roadLink	OGC:RailRoadSegment	0,58
OS:roadLink	OGC:RailRoadStation	0,58

4   Analysis of Machine Generated Similarity Values

Since the objective of generating similarity values is to assist in human based mapping and semi-automate the process of transformations, we need to analyze the generated values vis-à-vis human generated values of similarity in the absence of any assisting tool. The purpose here is to get an overview of how good the generated values are and also the presence of errors (which we shall group as false positives and false negatives)

4.1   Human Generated Similarity Values

The human generated similarity values were obtained by a small experiment. A blank similarity matrix sheet, class-attribute list and the class diagrams of the ontologies *A* and *T* (Appendix) were made available to the subject. Three steps were followed

(i)   A score of similarity (binary value) was recorded for every class name of the target with respect to each class name of the target based on English meaning of the words.

(ii)   Two scores of similarity (binary values) were recorded for every class name of the target with respect to each class name of the target based on its position in the class structure. The first score is reflective of the subclass occurring in the class structure. Thus a class in the Target with same number of child classes and attributes as another class in the Source will have a higher score. The Second score is reflective of the superclass and hence if the target ontology superclass contains same number of attributes as the source ontology, it results in a higher score.

(iii) The three scores which are recorded in the similarity matrix sheet are combined to obtain the most similar class and attributes. The basis of combination is not fixed but left to the judgment of the human so that if he/she feels that the English meaning of the word is more important for matching, the values of subclass structure and superclass structure can be ignore. By default an average of the three is taken.

4.2 Performance Parameters

We can now compare the performance of our machine generated similarity values. Graph 1 shows the difference in similarity values expressed as percentages. It should be remembered that the granularity of the human generated values is lower. Therefore it is more important to decide upon thresholds for the machine generated values in order to compare the two. Table 4, on the other hand, summarizes the top 10 class

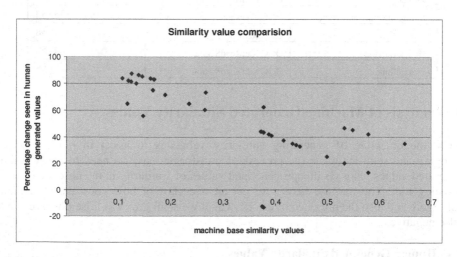

Graph 1. Percentage difference of human and machine based similarity values. We can see that there is higher percentage change among lower values of machine based similarity.

matches obtained from the human based similarity values. The numbers in italics are machine generated values lower than the threshold limits discussed.

False Positives: False Positives can be identified from the faulty values of the machine generated values. In our case this was 12.3% at t threshold of 0.50 and 36.9% at a threshold of 0.40. False positives were mainly seen in the cases where parts of the target class name existed as a part of the source class name.

False Negatives: Table 4 below shows the top ten class matches. The lower three cases have low machine generated values which indicate that such matches would not quality for mapping between the schemas. Overall Percentage of False negatives has been observed to be 4% at a threshold of 0.30 although the occurrence is higher(25%) in the top 20 class matches based on human generated similarity values.

Table 4. Top ten matches based on human generated similarity values

Target Class	Source Class	Machine Similarity
(c_{Tq})	(c_{Sp})	(cm_{SpTq})
OS:roadLink	RailRoadRoute	0,58
OS:roadLink	RailRoadSegment	0,58
OS:roadMember	RailRoadStation	0,58
OS:road	RailRoadRoute	0,55
OS:roadMember	RoadLinearFeatureEvent	0,533333
OS:roadLink	TransportationPath	0,377778
OS:ferryTerminal	TransferCluster	*0,267436*
OS:roadLink	LinearFeatureEvent	*0,169114*
OS:ferryTerminal	RailRoadRoute	*0,168297*

5 Data Translations Based on Ontology Mappings

Ontology mappings discussed in the previous sections are generated with a purpose to allow a framework to translate or extract the database records from a particular source database (and hence its schema elements) into that of another database (the target). Such a framework needs to include

- Translation of the query originating from a certain target database in terms of the schema elements of the source database based on ontology mappings of these elements.
- Similar translation of the results from the source into the schema elements of the target.

Both these points can be achieved using a wrapper based mechanism based on Xpath statements as shown in Figure 6 below. This approach is similar to the approach

```
- <gml:FeatureCollection
      xmlns:osgb="http://www.ordnancesurvey.co.uk/xml/namespaces/o
      sgb" xmlns:gml="http://www.opengis.net/gml"
      xmlns:xlink="http://www.w3.org/1999/xlink"
      xmlns:xsi="http://www.w3.org/2001/XMLSchema-instance"
      xsi:schemaLocation="http://www.ordnancesurvey.co.uk/xml/namesp
      aces/osgb/schema" xmlns:ogc="http://www.opengis.net/ogcl">
  - <OGCGMLSIMPLE1>
    - <BaseTransportation_GML3L0>
          { for $TranPath in //RoadSeg return
          <TranPath fid="{$TranPath/@fid}" />
          } { for $TranPath in //RoadPoint return
          <TranPath fid="{$TranPath/@fid}" />
          } { for $TranPoint in //RoadPath return
          <TranPoint fid="{$TranPoint/@fid}" />
          } { for $TranPoint in //RoadSeg return
          <TranPoint fid="{$TranPoint/@fid}" />
          } { for $TranSeg in //RoadPath return
          <TranSeg fid="{$TranSeg/@fid}" />
          } { for $TranSeg in //RoadSeg return
          <TranSeg fid="{$TranSeg/@fid}" />
          } { for $TranSeg in //RoadPoint return
          <TranSeg fid="{$TranSeg/@fid}" />
          }
      </BaseTransportation_GML3L0>
      <Roads_GML3L0 />
  </OGCGMLSIMPLE1>
</gml:FeatureCollection>
```

Fig. 6. XQuery based Wrapper generated from ontology mapping

discussed by based on the ontology mapping and allows data to extracted from the source into the target. However, this framework assumes XML enabled databases.

Geographic Markup Language (GML)[1] supported data allows the use of XQuery statements and a sample translation of data from one (source)database to another (target) database is shown below. The figure 7 shows maps rendered from the source data and the translated version. Since the geometric data remains unchanged in the ontology mapping, changes can be seen in the attribute properties of the data classes seen in the *properties window*.

The translation is based on the following principles:

(i)   Data records belonging to a class, which maps to another class in the target database, are reported as members of the mapped class.
(ii) If the class is a part of another class and the target class is constituted as a join or manipulation[3] of record values from the source data class.

---

[3] Although manipulation could include transformation of data structures such as string to integer, in this case we mean manipulations, which transform the data without additional information such as multiplication factor or addition/deletion of a constant value. manipulation formula although we have not used the same.

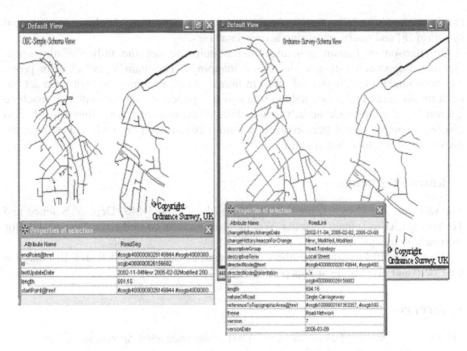

Fig. 7. GML data from Source and translated version displayed along with class attributes

6 Conclusions and Future Work

We have seen that lexical similarities of schema element labels and descriptions can help in ontology mapping. Along with similarity propagation based on heuristics allows integration of implicit semantics of the ontology structure and hence improves the mapping process. The propagation of similarity is directional in nature as opposed previous approaches [5,8,9]. However the experiments have also shown that there are problems with machine based similarity assessment.

(i) Thesemantic similarity of individual words does not always provide a good indicator of the semantic similarity of group words. Since class descriptions were used for similarity assessment this led to false positives in many cases.

(ii) Similarly although limited word senses were evaluated based on part of speech, word sense disambiguation would help to reduce number of false negatives. Such cases explain the occurrence of high percentage change of human generated similarity values among lower values machine generated values

It is also important to note that use of heuristics and threshold values is critical in order to use the semi-automatic mapping approach.

These are only the initial results from our efforts to allow transformations based on a semi-automated approach as discussed in the motivation. The translation of data from the source to the target as shown in § 5 is only a step towards a broader framework of interoperable databases using ontologies. The whole exercise of ontology mapping can be seen in the context of ontology aware database management systems [18] and query answering across databases.

Comparison of human generated values helps to see the utility of the semi-automated approach with machine based mappings. The main aspect of error prone and non-standard techniques followed in human based matching has not been set out forth in this paper and is beyond the scope of this paper. We can assume that machine generated values provide an advantage. Future work in this area, therefore, has to involve a comparison of performance in human based mapping with and without the assistance of machine-based values.

Acknowledgments

The work presented in this paper is supported by the NRDMS, Dept of Science and Technology, Government of India. We are also thankful to Ordnance Survey, UK for their help in this project.

We are grateful to other members of the team at CSE and CSRE, IIT Bombay for their help and discussions in this project.

References

1. OGC: Geography Markup Language (GML) Implementation Specification, Version 3.0 2003, (last visited 22.04.2006) available at http://www.opengeospatial.org/docs/02-023r4.pdf
2. Lutz, M., Klien, E.: Ontology-Based Retrieval of Geographic Information. International Journal of Geographical Information Science 20(3), 233–260 (2006)
3. Gruber, T.R: Toward Principles for the Design of Ontologies Used for Knowledge Sharing. In: Formal Ontology in Conceptual Analysis and Knowledge Representation, Kluwer Academic Publishers, Dordrecht (1993)
4. Sen, S., Somavarapu, S., Sarda, N.L.: Resolving Semantic Heterogeneity in the Indian NSDI: An Ontology Mapping Approach. In: Proc. of MapIndia Conference, New Delhi (2006)
5. Melnik, S., Garcia-Molina, H., Rahm, E.: Similarity flooding: A versatile graph matching algorithm. In: Proceedings of the International Conference on Data Engineering (ICDE), pp. 117–128 (2002)
6. Shvaiko, P.: A Classification of Schema-based Matching Approaches. In: McIlraith, S.A., Plexousakis, D., van Harmelen, F. (eds.) ISWC 2004. LNCS, vol. 3298. Springer, Heidelberg (2004)
7. Fellbaum, C. (ed.): WordNet - An Electronic Lexical Database. The MIT Press, Cambridge (1999)
8. Melnik, S., Rahm, E., Bernstein, P.A.: Rondo: A Programming Platform for Model Management. In: Proc. ACM SIGMOD 2003, San Diego (June 2003)
9. Madhavan, J., Bernstein, P.A., Rahm, E.: Generic Schema Matching Using Cupid. In: Proc. VLDB 2001(PDF, 140KB) Extended version: MSR-TR-2001-58 (2001)
10. Noy, N.F.: Semantic Integration: A Survey Of Ontology-Based Approaches SIGMOD Record. Special Issue on Semantic Integration 33(4) (December 2004)
11. Halevy, A.Y., Ives, G.I., Mork, P., Tatarinov, I.: Data Management Infrastructure for Semantic Web Applications. IEEE Transactions on Knowledge and Data Engineering 16(7), 787–798 (2004)
12. Doan, A., Madhavan, J., Domingos, P., Halevy, A.: Learning to map between ontologies on the semantic web. In: The Eleventh International WWW Conference, Hawaii, US (2002)

13. Giunchiglia, F., Shvaiko, P.: Semantic Matching. The Knowledge Engineering Review Journal 18(3), 265–280 (2003)
14. Bishr, Y.: Semantic aspects of interoperable GIS. In: Ph.D. Dissertation, International Institute for Aerospace Survey and Earth Sciences, Enschede, The Netherlands, p. 154. ITC Publication No. 56 (1997)
15. Evens, M., Smith, R.: Properties of Lexical Semantic Relations. The Finite String, No. 4 (1978)
16. Ordnance Survey: Ordnance Survey OS MasterMap Integrated Transport Network (ITN) Layer available at http://www.ordnancesurvey.co.uk/oswebsite/products/osmastermap/itn/ (last visited 22.04.2006)
17. Cruz, I.F., Rajendran, A.: Semantic Data Integration in Hierarchial Domains. IEEE Intelligent Systems 18(2), 66–73 (2003)
18. Sarda, N.L.: Ontology-aware database management systems. In: Proceedings of IRMA International conference, Philadelphia (2003)

Appendix: Ontologies from the geospatial domain used for the case study.

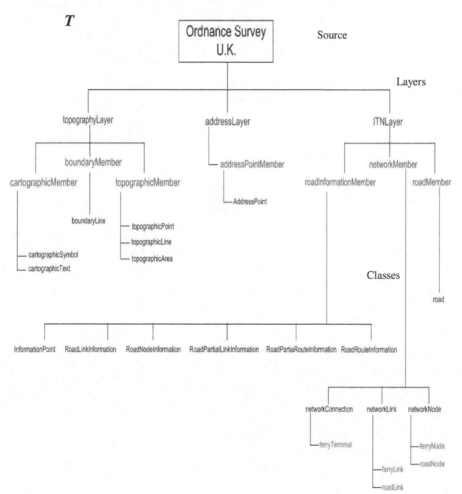

A

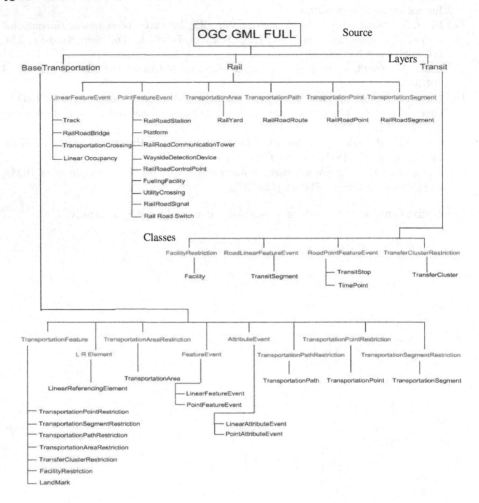

Scalable Interoperability Through the Use of COIN Lightweight Ontology

Hongwei Zhu[1,2] and Stuart E. Madnick[1]

[1] Massachusetts Institute of Technology
Sloan School of Management
30 Wadsworth Street, E53-320, Cambridge, MA 02142, USA
{mrzhu,smadnick}@mit.edu
[2] Old Dominion University
College of Business and Public Administration
Constant 2079, Norfolk, VA 23529, USA
hzhu@odu.edu

Abstract. There are many different kinds of ontologies used for different purposes in modern computing. A continuum exists from lightweight ontologies to formal ontologies. In this paper we compare and contrast the lightweight ontology and the formal ontology approaches to data interoperability. Both approaches have strengths and weaknesses, but they both lack scalability because of the n^2 problem. We present an approach that combines their strengths and avoids their weaknesses. In this approach, the ontology includes only high level concepts; subtle differences in the interpretation of the concepts are captured as context descriptions outside the ontology. The resulting ontology is simple, thus it is easy to create. It also provides a structure for context descriptions. The structure can be exploited to facilitate automatic composition of context mappings. This mechanism leads to a scalable solution to semantic interoperability among disparate data sources and contexts.

Keywords: lightweight ontology, formal ontology, context, mediation, scalability, semantic heterogeneity.

1 Introduction

Ontologies have been widely used in modern computing for purposes such as communication, computational inference, and knowledge organization and reuse [7]. For different purposes there are a variety of different ontologies, which range from a glossary, to a taxonomy, a database schema, or a full-fledged logic theory that consists of concepts, relationships, constraints, axioms, and inference machinery. As illustrated in [21], a variety of ontologies form a continuum from lightweight, rather informal, to heavyweight, and formal ontologies.

The lightweight ontology approach and the formal ontology approach are often used differently and have different strengths and weaknesses. Both approaches can be used to support data interoperability among disparate sources.

M. Collard (Ed.): ODBIS 2005/2006, LNCS 4623, pp. 37–50, 2007.

Lightweight ontologies usually are taxonomies, which consist of a set of concepts (i.e., terms, or semantic types) and hierarchical relationships among the concepts. As an artifact, it is relatively easy to construct a lightweight ontology. However, such lightweight ontologies do not capture the detailed semantics of the concepts, which sometimes is documented in a data dictionary, and/or embedded in the data models and the data processing programs.

There are two different approaches to using lightweight ontologies for interoperability purposes. One approach is to develop a single lightweight ontology, in which case all parties need to agree on the exact meaning of the concepts. The lightweight ontology and the agreements together form a standard that all parties uniformly adopt and implement. That is, a lightweight ontology is often used to support strict data standardization. However, reaching such agreements can be difficult. For example, a data standardization effort within the U.S. Department of Defense (DoD) took more than a decade only to standardize less than 2% of the data across all organizations of the DoD [18]. The alternative approach is to allow multiple lightweight ontologies to co-exist, in which case mappings among the ontologies need to be provided. Because the semantics is not formally captured in the ontologies, efforts are required to identify the semantic differences and then develop (often hand-code) the mappings to enable pair-wise interoperability. The number of pair-wise mappings is $n(n-1)$ (which is $O(n^2)$) if there are n different ontologies, thus the amount of effort required increases quickly as n becomes large. This is the so called n^2 problem of data interoperability. A survey [19] shows that approximately 70% of the costs of data interoperability projects are spent on identifying the semantic differences and developing code to reconcile them.

In contrast, the formal ontology approach uses axioms to explicitly represent semantics and has inference capabilities. This approach can also support interoperability either via a single ontology or via mappings of multiple ontologies. The key difference is that the semantics of the ontological concepts and the mappings are explicitly captured in a formal logic theory.

To summarize, both ontology approaches can be used to support data interoperability either via standardization or via mappings of multiple ontologies. The difficulty of reaching an agreement on a single data standard can be enormous so that in practice multiple standards (i.e., ontologies) co-exist even within a single organization. Thus, in practice ontology mappings are required to enable interoperability among data sources and systems. Both ontology approaches suffer from the n^2 problem. The key difference between the two ontology approaches is that lightweight ontologies do not capture the semantics in the ontologies, whereas formal ontologies explicitly capture semantics. As artifacts, lightweight ontologies are simple and easy to create, whereas formal ontologies are complex and difficult to create. But the semantics and the mappings of lightweight ontologies are often scattered in various data models and data processing programs, making maintenance extremely difficult. The semantics and mappings of formal ontologies are in the form of a logic theory, which is relatively easier to maintain. Both approaches have weaknesses that limit their effectiveness.

It is desirable to have an approach that combines the strengths and avoid the weaknesses of the two ontological approaches. In this paper, we present such an approach, which is developed in the COntext INterchange (COIN) project [3, 5, 25] for semantic data interoperation purposes. It uses a lightweight ontology, which provides the structure for organizing context descriptions to account for the subtleties of the concepts in the ontology. We will use the terms *COIN ontology* and *COIN lightweight ontology* interchangeably. COIN also implements a reasoning algorithm to determine and reconcile semantic differences between different data sources and receivers.

The rest of the paper is organized as follows. In Section 2, we describe the COIN lightweight ontology approach. In Section 3, we present the scalability benefit of the approach. In Section 4, we discuss related work. In Section 5, we conclude and point out future research.

2   COIN Lightweight Ontology

We will use an online price comparison example to illustrate the COIN lightweight ontology approach.

2.1   Online Price Comparison Example

Numerous vendors make their pricing information available online. With web wrappers, such as Cameleon [2] and others [1], and the increasing adoption of XML and web services, one can gather price data and compare offers from different vendors. To perform meaningful comparisons, one has to reconcile the semantic differences of price data, especially when data is from vendors scattered around the world [22].

Consider a scenario where data is from 30 vendors from 10 different countries. For simplicity of discussion in this paper, let us assume that all vendors quote prices using the same schema and same *Product* identification, represented using the following first order predicate:

$$quote(Product, Price, Date)$$

but different vendors use different conventions so that the price values are interpreted differently depending on which vendor provides the quote. Table 1 provides a few examples of different interpretations of price. A *base price* refers to price with taxes and shipping & handling (S&H) excluded (e.g., price quotes from vendors 2 and 3).

Let us assume that each vendor uses a different convention, thus we have 30 unique conventions, which we call *contexts*. We can label vendor i's context as c_i. For

Table 1. Interpretations of Price

Vendor	Interpretation of Price
1	In 1's of USD, taxes and S&H included
2	In 1's of USD, taxes and S&H excluded
3	In thousands of Korean won, taxes and S&H excluded
...	...
30	In millions of Turkish lira, taxes included

simplicity, we will assume that users normally adopt a vendor context. Or we can assume that the only users are the vendors, each of whom wants to compare his prices with all of his world-wide competitors and wants the comparison done in his own context. In this scenario, to allow users in all contexts to meaningfully compare vendor prices, it is necessary that price data from other contexts be converted to the user context, which would require 870 (i.e., 30*29=870) conversions. Hand-coding these conversions and maintaining them over time, since contexts do change (e.g., prices in French francs and German deutschemarks became Euros), can be costly and error-prone.

2.2 COIN Lightweight Ontology

In the example, there are a number of subtle differences in the meaning of the high level concept *price*. It is important that these subtleties are captured and the differences are reconciled for meaningful comparisons.

Like the traditional lightweight ontology, the COIN ontology includes a set of concepts, among which there can be a hierarchy represented with an *is_a* relationship. Besides, the COIN ontology also includes *attribute* as a binary relationship between a pair of concepts. Attributes are also called roles, and correspondingly attribute names are called role names. For example, *price* can be the *hasPrice* attribute of *product*. Conversely, *product* can be the *priceOf* attribute of *price*. To capture the subtle differences in meaning, the COIN lightweight ontology introduces *modifier* as a special kind of attribute. The values of modifiers are specified as context descriptions outside the ontology. Fig. 1 shows a graphic representation of the COIN lightweight ontology for the online price comparison example.

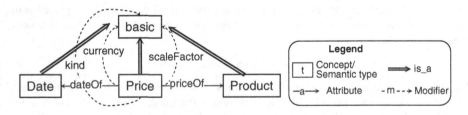

Fig. 1. COIN lightweight ontology for online price comparison example. It contains only high level concepts, the refined variants of which can be derived from the assignments of modifiers that belong to each high level concept.

In this ontology, we include a modifier-free root concept *basic*, which is similar to *thing* as the root in many object-oriented models. We include three modifiers: *kind*, *currency*, and *scaleFactor*. Each modifier captures a particular aspect in which the underlying concept can have different interpretations. Contexts are described by assigning values to modifiers present in the ontology. In simple cases, a specific value is assigned to a modifier in a context. In other cases, the assignment must be specified by a set of rules. In either case, a context is conceptually a set of assignments of all modifiers and can be described by a set of <*modifier, value*> pairs. For example, contexts c_2 and c_3 (refer to vendors 2 and 3 in Table 1) can be described as:

$$c_2 := \{ \ <kind, basePrice>, \qquad c_3 := \{ \ <kind, basePrice>,$$
$$<currency, usd>, \qquad\qquad <currency, krw>,$$
$$<scaleFactor, 1> \} \qquad\qquad <scaleFactor, 1000> \}$$

The language used in COIN for describing context (as well as context mappings and the lightweight ontology) is based on F-logic [12], an object-oriented logic. F-logic rules are converted to Datalog for reasoning purposes. In COIN, various "user-friendly" front-ends have been created so that developers do not directly need to use F-logic or Datalog. Below is example rule using the logic to assign a value to *currency* modifier in context c_3:

$$\forall X : price \ \exists Y : basic \vdash$$
$$X[currency(c_3) \rightarrow Y] \wedge Y[value(c_3) \rightarrow 'KRW'].$$

where variables (e.g., X, Y) are objects, the modifier and attributes of which are represented by methods (which are declared in square brackets). The method *value* is similar to the *value* predicate in context logic of [15]; it returns the ground value of the object in the context specified by the parameter (which is c_3 in the example).

2.3 Characteristics of COIN Lightweight Ontology

A COIN ontology, as shown in Fig. 1, includes only high level concepts (plus their relationships, such as the binary relationships of context modifiers). Thus it is simple and relatively easy to create and reach agreement. But the involved parties do not need to agree on the details of each concept. Each party can continue to use its preferred interpretation for each high level concept. In other words, each party can *conceptually* have its own local ontology. Fig. 2 depicts the conceptual local ontologies for vendors 2 and 3. To avoid clutter, we have omitted attribute names in the figure.

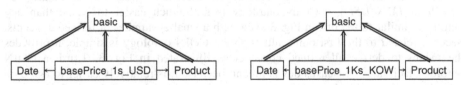

Fig. 2. Conceptual local ontologies for vendor 2 (left) and vendor 3 (right), derivable from COIN lightweight ontology shown in Fig. 1

These local ontologies are not part of the COIN lightweight ontology, but they can be derived from the COIN ontology using the context descriptions. In other words, the COIN lightweight ontology provides a structured way to describe contexts and derive refined local ontologies.

Furthermore, a more traditional global ontology that integrates all the local ontologies could be constructed from the COIN ontology and the accompanying context descriptions. A graphic representation of such a global ontology for the online price comparison example is given in Fig. 3, which includes two intermediate layers (i.e., the layers starting with *BasePrice* and *In USD* concepts, respectively). Concepts in each layer remove a certain kind of ambiguity. For example, *BasePrice* indicates the kind of price, which does not include shipping and handling charges. The nodes below it further refine the base price concept by specifying the currency, e.g., in USD. Alternatively, the intermediate layers can be omitted. In this case, specialized concepts on the leaf level, such as *basePrice_1s_USD*, directly connect to the generic *Price* concept.

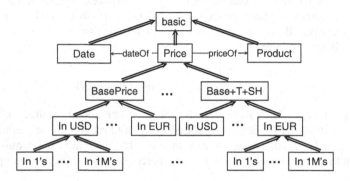

Fig. 3. An example fully-specified global ontology for the online price comparison example. Leaf nodes represents the concepts with specific semantics, e.g., the first leaf node on the left represent the concept of "price, not including taxes or shipping handling, in 1's of USD".

Ontologies are design artifacts. Comparing the artifacts shown in Fig. 1 and Fig. 3, we observe that the COIN approach creates much simpler ontologies – though, for many purposes, they are functionally equivalent. As discussed in [13, 24], the COIN approach has several advantages over the formal ontology approach. First, the COIN ontology is usually much simpler, thus easier to manage. Although in practice it is unlikely that one would create an ontology to include all possible variations (e.g., *basePrice_1M's_USD*), a COIN ontology is still much easier to create than any ontology similar to the one in Fig. 3 even with a smaller number of refined concepts. Second, related to the first point, although the COIN ontology is simple, it provides the means to derive all refined concepts as illustrated in Fig. 3. Third, a COIN ontology facilitates consensus development, because it is relatively easier to agree on a small set of high level concepts than to agree on every piece of detail of a large set of fine-grained concepts. And more importantly, the COIN ontology is much more adaptable to changes. For example, when a new concept "base price + S&H in 1000's of South Korean Won" is needed, the fully specified ontology may need to be updated with insertions of new nodes. The update requires the approval of all parties who agreed on the initial ontology if a single ontology is used, or mappings need to be added to ensure its interoperability with other variants of the *price* concept. In contrast, the COIN approach can accommodate this new concept by adding new context descriptions without changing the ontology. As we will see later, the new mappings may not need to be added when they can be derived from existing mappings using a reasoning mechanism.

The COIN lightweight ontology approach also has advantages over the traditional lightweight ontology approach. Although, similar to the traditional approach, the

COIN ontology does not include detailed descriptions of semantics, it does provide a vocabulary and the structure for describing semantics using context descriptions. As we will see in the next section, the context reasoning mechanism exploits the structure to solve the n^2 problem.

3 Scalable Interoperability with COIN Lightweight Ontology

When data sources and data receivers are in different contexts, conversions (also called lifting rules or mappings) are needed to convert data from source contexts to the receiver context. We call the set of conversions from a context to another context a *composite conversion*. When conversions are specified pair-wise between contexts, it requires ~n^2 composite conversions to achieve interoperability among n contexts. It is costly and error-prone to develop and maintain such a large number of conversions. Thus approaches that hand-code the ~n^2 composite conversions do not scale well when n increases.

The use of lightweight ontology in COIN makes it possible to avoid the above mentioned problem. In addition to using ontology and contexts to represent semantic heterogeneity, COIN also has a reasoning component to determine and reconcile semantic differences. We explain how COIN achieves scalability though conversion composition in the remainder of the section.

3.1 Conversion Composition

In COIN, conversions are not specified as convoluted rules pair-wise between contexts. Instead, they are specified for each modifier between different modifier values. For example, a conversion can be defined for *currency* modifier to convert values in different currencies such as by using an exchange rate function represented by the following predicate:

$$olsen(CurFrom, CurTo, Day, Rate)$$

It returns an exchange *Rate* from *CurFrom* currency to *CurTo* currency on a given *Day*. The function can be implemented externally as a table lookup or as a callable service[1]. We call a conversion defined for a single modifier a *component conversion*.

The component conversions in COIN are also specified using F-logic. Below is an example component conversion for currency modifier; it is parameterized with context C1 and C2 and can convert between any currencies. We use *olsen_* for the skolemized version of original *olsen* predicate.

$$\forall X : price \vdash$$
$$X[cvt(currency, C2) @ C1, u \rightarrow v] \leftarrow$$
$$X[currency(C1) \rightarrow C_f] \wedge X[currency(C2) \rightarrow C_t] \wedge x[dataOf \rightarrow T] \wedge$$
$$olsen\_(A,B,R,D) \wedge C_f \overset{C2}{=} A \wedge C_t \overset{C2}{=} B \wedge T \overset{C2}{=} D \wedge R[value(C2) \rightarrow r] \wedge v = u * r.$$

---

[1] In many applications using COIN, such conversion functions are implemented by using web wrapped services, such as the www.oanda.com currency conversion web site.

Once all component conversions are defined, composite conversions can be composed automatically using a context reasoning algorithm. Fig. 4 illustrates the concept of conversion composition.

In Fig. 4, the triangle symbol on the left represents the price concept in context c_3, i.e., base price in 1000's of South Korean won (KRW); and the circle symbol on the right represents the price concept in context c_2, i.e., base price in 1's of USD. For data in context c_3 to be viewed in context c_2, they need to be appropriately converted by applying the appropriate composite conversion. The dashed straight arrow represents the application of the composite conversion that would have been implemented manually in other approaches. With the COIN lightweight ontology approach, the composite conversion can be automatically composed using the predefined component conversions. As shown in Fig. 4, we first apply the component conversion for *currency* modifier (represented by cvt$_{currency}$), then apply the component conversion for *scaleFactor* modifier (represented by cvt$_{scaleFactor}$).

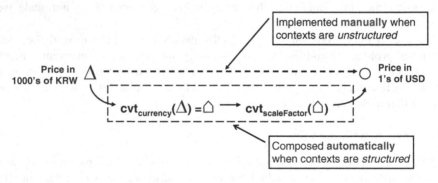

Fig. 4. Composite conversion composed using component conversions. Without composition, one would hand-code a direct conversion to convert the price in 1000's of KRW to the price in 1's of USD; this conversion illustrated by the straight dashed arrow. With COIN, this composite conversion can be derived from the component conversions for currency (cvt$_{currency}$) and scale factor (cvt$_{scaleFactor}$).

The composition algorithm, shown in Fig. 5, is quite simple. In COIN project, it is implemented in a query rewriting mediator using abductive constraint logic programming (ACLP) [10] and constraint handling rules (CHR) [4]. With the mediator, queries can be issued as if all data sources were in the requester's context (i.e., the target context). The mediator generates mediated queries that contain the composite conversions. Data is converted from source contexts to the requester's context when the mediated queries are executed.

A demonstration of the query mediator is shown in Fig. 6. The source used also includes a *Vendor* column, as shown in the sample schema near the middle of the figure. The source context corresponds to context c_3, and the requester context (c_c_usa2 in the figure) is equivalent to context c_2 in the online price comparison example discussed earlier. In the demonstration, the *QuoteDate* field can have different date formats, which we did not include in the ontology discussed earlier but can be accommodated by adding a *dateFormat* modifier to *Date* concept in the ontology in Fig. 1.

```
Input: data value V, corresponding concept C in ontology,
       source context C1, target context C2
Output: data value V (interpretable in context C2)

Find all modifiers of C
  For each modifier mi
       Find and compare mi's values in C1 and C2
       If different: V=cvt_mi(V); else, V=V
Return V
```

Fig. 5. Algorithm for composing composite conversion using component conversions

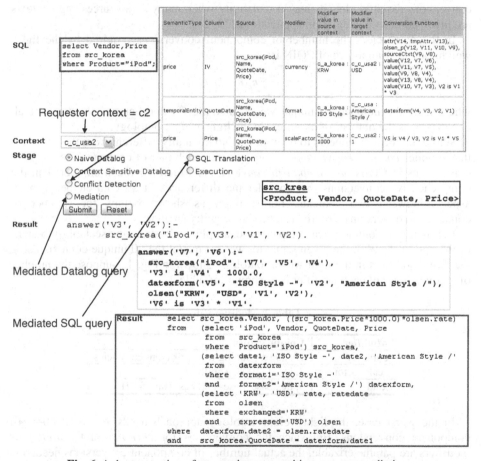

Fig. 6. A demonstration of conversion composition as query mediation

The requester SQL query, shown in the upper left of the figure, need not be aware of any context differences. Our demonstration system allows us to step through the various steps of mediation individually (e.g., converting the SQL to naïve Datalog query, etc.). The Conflict Detection step outputs a table that summarizes the concepts (called Semantic Types) whose modifiers have different values in the source and requester contexts. A mediated Datalog query is generated using the algorithm shown in Fig. 5. As can be seen, the mediated query contains the necessary conversions to reconcile the context differences (namely currency and scale factor differences of *price* concept, which corresponds to the Price filed in the source table, and format difference of the *Date* concept, which corresponds to the *QuoteDate* field). The mediated Datalog query can be converted an SQL query, which is shown at the bottom in the figure.

3.2 Scalability Benefit

The primary benefit of the composition capability is the small number of component conversions required, thus increased scalability when many data sources and contexts are involved in data integration applications [23, 24].

In the worst case, the number of component conversions required by the light-weight ontology approach of COIN is:

$$\sum_{i=1}^{m} n_i (n_i - 1)$$

where n_i is the number of unique values that the ith modifier has to represent all contexts, m is the number of modifiers in the light-weight ontology.

While the formula appears to be n^2, it is fundamentally different from the approach that supplies *comprehensive conversions* between each pair of contexts. The supplied conversions in COIN are *component conversions,* which are much simpler than the comprehensive conversions that consider the differences of all data elements in all aspects between two contexts. Furthermore, as shown below, the number of component conversions required can be significantly smaller.

Let us use the online price comparison example to illustrate the scalability benefit of the approach. With the given scenario, we can model the 30 unique contexts using the three modifiers in the light-weight ontology shown in Fig. 1. Suppose the number of unique values of each modifier is as shown in Table 2.

Table 2. Modifier values

Modifier	Unique values
currency	10, corresponding to 10 different currencies
scaleFactor	3, i.e., 1, 1000, 1 million
kind	3, i.e., base, base+tax, base+tax+S&H

In the worst case, the light-weight ontology approach needs 102 (i.e., 90+6+6) component conversions. But since the conversions for *currency* and *scaleFactor* modifiers are parameterizable, the actual number of component conversions needed is further reduced to 8, which is a significant improvement from the 870 composite conversions required when conversions are specified pair-wise between contexts.

The number of component conversions can be further reduced when equational relationships exist between contexts with different values of a modifier. Symbolic equation solver techniques have been developed to exploit such relationships [3]. For example, consider the three definitions for price: (A) base price, (B) price with tax included, and (C) price with tax and shipping & handling included. With known equational relationships among the three price definitions, and two component conversions:

(1) from base_price to base_price+tax (i.e., A to B) and
(2) from base_price+tax to base_price + tax + shipping & handling (i.e., B to C)

the symbolic equation solver can compute the other four conversions automatically (A to C and the three inverses). This technique further reduces the number of component conversions needed for a modifier from $n_i(n_i-1)$ to (n_i-1).

In many cases, the component conversion for a modifier can be parameterized, i.e., the component conversion can be applied to convert for any given pair of modifier values. In this case, we only need to supply one component conversion for the modifier, regardless of the number of unique values that the modifier may have. The exchange rate function given earlier is such an example; with it, we only need one component conversion for the *currency* modifier.

We use Fig. 7 to illustrate the intuition of the scalability result.

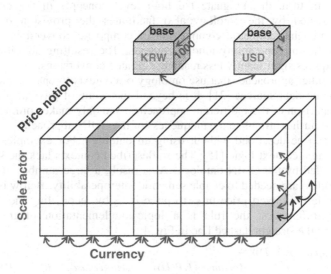

Fig. 7. Intuition of scalability of COIN approach. Component conversions are provided along the modifier axes. Composite conversions between any cubes in the space can be automatically composed.

The modifiers of each ontological concept span a context space within which the variants of the concept exist. Each modifier defines a dimension. In the figure, we show the space spanned by the three modifiers of *price* concept. The component conversions required by the COIN approach are defined along the axes of the modifiers. With the composition capability, the COIN approach can automatically generate all the conversions between units (e.g., the cubes in a three-dimensional space, as sown in Fig. 7) in the space using the component conversions along the dimensions. In contrast, the approaches that suffer from the n^2 problem require the conversions between any two units in the space to be supplied.

4 Related Work and Discussion

The most commonly cited definition for ontology is given in [6], where an ontology is a "formal explicit specification of a share conceptualization". But as discussed in [7, 20], there is not a consensus definition for ontology, and there are many types of ontologies, some of which use formal logic to explicitly capture the intended meanings, and others use a set of mutually agreed terms to provide a shared taxonomy. In the latter case, the intended meanings are not explicitly captured in the ontology, rather, they are implicitly captured in the agreement.

The term *lightweight ontology* has been used very loosely in the literature. Generally speaking, a lightweight ontology refers to a set of concepts organized in a hierarchy with *is_a* relationships. Data dictionaries, product catalogs, and topic maps are often considered to be lightweight ontologies. Opposite to lightweight ontologies are formal ontologies, which often use formal logic to specify constraints, relationships, and other rules that apply to the concepts [8, 14].

The use of ontology and contexts in the COIN approach is quite unique. The ontology provides the necessary structure for context descriptions; and the context descriptions, in turn, disambiguate the high level concepts in the ontology. The structure provided by the ontology also facilitates the provision of component conversions and the automatic composition of composite conversions necessary to enable semantic interoperability among contexts. The resulting solution is scalable because it requires significantly less manually created conversions.

There are other approaches that use ontology or contexts to enable interoperability among disparate data sources [21]. It is beyond the scope of this paper to provide a detailed comparison of these different approaches. We only make comments on a few approaches to further articulate the uniqueness of the COIN approach.

Contexts can be described without using an ontology. For example, they can be described using a context logic [15]. The so described contexts lack the structure like the one provided by the COIN ontology. As a result, a large number of conversions (i.e., lifting rules) are needed to enable semantic interoperability. Below is an example conversion rule to convert price in c_3 to price in c_2 by reconciling the currency and scale factor differences; the rule is a logic implementation of the conversion represented by the straight dashed line in Fig. 4:

$$c_0 : ist(c_2, quote(I, X, D)) \leftarrow$$
$$ist(c_3, quote(I, P, D)), \quad olsen(krw, usd, D, R), X = P * R * 1000.$$

Suppose there n cubes in the contextual space shown in Fig. 7, the approach requires $n(n-1)$ conversion rules like the above one to enable full interoperability.

A recent effort tries to categorize lifting rules and attempts to use the patterns revealed to devise general lifting rules [9]. More work is needed to show how these patterns help with creation of general lifting rules and how these rules can be applied to reason with multiple contexts.

Ontology is used in [16], where all types of data level and schema level heterogeneity in multiple data sources are explicitly represented using a semantic conflict resolution ontology (SCROL). For example, when acres and square meters are used in different sources to represent the *area* of a parcel of land, the SCROL ontology will explicitly represent the semantic difference by including two sub-concepts of area: *area_in_acre*, and *area_in_sq_meter*. A SCROL ontology resembles the one in Fig. 3. The ontology needs to be updated when a new kind of heterogeneity is introduced, e.g., "area in square miles". No characterization on the number of conversions needed is given in the paper.

Ontology is also used in [11] to provide structured context representation for purposes of data interoperability in a multi-database environment. However, we are not certain if their ontology would constitute a lightweight ontology. Nor does the paper provide an assessment about the number of conversions required.

5 Conclusion

The COIN lightweight ontology approach to semantic interoperability has several advantages. The ontology is simple, thus it is easy to create. The semantics of the concepts is described as context descriptions outside the ontology. It can be as a hybrid approach where are a lightweight ontology is annotated with a logic (i.e., F-logic) that can be in a formal ontology approach. The use of modifiers to capture subtle meaning differences provides the structure for describing the subtleties, and facilitates the provision of component conversions, with which any composite conversions can be composed dynamically to reconcile the semantic differences between the sources and the receivers of data.

For future research, we would like to explore the applicability of the COIN approach in other application domains, such as context-aware web services and peer-to-peer information sharing. Another promising area is to apply the context represent-tation and reasoning techniques to Semantic Web applications. Initial work has been done [19] to represent COIN ontology and contexts using Semantic Web languages, such as OWL and RuleML. The preliminary results indicate that COIN lightweight ontology, structured context descriptions, and component lifting rules can be represented using Semantic Web languages. Future work will adapt the reasoning algorithm and evaluate its performance at large scales that are typical on the Semantic Web.

Acknowledgements. This work has been supported, in part, by The MITRE Corporation, the MIT-Malaysia University of Science and Technology (MUST) project, the Singapore-MIT Alliance (SMA), and Suruga Bank.

References

1. Chang, C.H., Kaye, M., Girgis, M.R., Shaalan, K.F.: A Survey of Web Information Extraction System. IEEE Transactions on Knowledge and Data Engineering 18(10), 1411–1428 (2006)
2. Firat, A., Madnick, S.E., Siegel, M.D.: The Cameleon Web Wrapper Engine. In: Workshop on Technologies for E-Services (TES'00), Cairo, Egypt (2000)
3. Firat, A.: Information Integration using Contextual Knowledge and Ontology Merging. In: PhD Thesis, Sloan School of Management. MIT, Cambridge, MA (2003)
4. Frühwirth, T.: Theory and Practice of Constraint Handling Rules. Journal of Logic Programming 37(1-3), 95–138 (1998)
5. Goh, C.H., Bressan, S., Madnick, S., Siegel, M.: Context Interchange: New Features and Formalisms for the Intelligent Integration of Information. ACM Transitions on Information Systems 17(3), 270–293 (1999)

6. Gruber, T.R.: A Translation Approach to Portable Ontology Specifications. Knowledge Acquisition 5(2), 199–220 (1993)
7. Gruninger, M., Lee, J.: Ontology Applications and Design. Communications of the ACM 45(2), 39–41 (2002)
8. Guarino, N.: Formal Ontology and Information Systems. In: Guarino, N. (ed.) Proceedings of Formal Ontologies in Information Systems (FOIS '98), Trento, Italy, June 6-8, 1998, pp. 3–15. IOS Press, Amsterdam (1998)
9. Guha, R., McCarthy, J.: Varieties of Contexts. In: Blackburn, P., Ghidini, C., Turner, R.M., Giunchiglia, F. (eds.) CONTEXT 2003. LNCS, vol. 2680, pp. 164–177. Springer, Heidelberg (2003)
10. Kakas, A.C., Michael, A., Mourlas, C.: ACLP: Abductive Constraint Logic Programming. Journal of Logic Programming 44(1-3), 129–177 (2000)
11. Kashyap, V., Sheth, A.P.: Semantic and Schematic Similarities between Database Objects: A Context-Based Approach. VLDB Journal 5(4), 276–304 (1996)
12. Kiffer, M., Laussen, G., Wu, J.: Logic Foundations of Object-Oriented and Frame-based Languages. J. ACM 42(4), 741–843 (1995)
13. Madnick, S.E., Zhu, H.: Improving data quality through effective use of data semantics. Data & Knowledge Engineering 59(2), 460–475 (2006)
14. Mädsche, A.: Ontology Learning for the Semantic Web. Kluwer Academic Publishers, Boston, MA (2002)
15. McCarthy, J., Buvac, S.: Formalizing Context (Expanded Notes). In: Aliseda, A., van Glabbeek, R., Westerstahl, D. (eds.) Computing natural language, Sanford University (1997)
16. Ram, S., Park, J.: Semantic Conflict Resolution Ontology (SCROL): An Ontology for Detecting and Resolving Data and Schema-Level Semantic Conflict. IEEE Transactions on Knowledge and Data Engineering 16(2), 189–202 (2004)
17. Rosenthal, A., Seligman, L., Renner, S.: From Semantic Integration to Semantics Management: Case Studies and a Way Forward. ACM SIGMOD Record 33(4), 44–50 (2004)
18. Seligman, L., Rosenthal, A., Lehner, P., Smith, A.: Data Integration: Where Does the Time Go? IEEE Bulletin of the Technical Committee on Data Engineering 25(3), 3–10 (2002)
19. Tan, P., Madnick, S.E., Tan, K.-L.: Context Mediation in the Semantic Web: Handling OWL Ontology and Data Disparity Through Context Interchange. In: Bussler, C.J., Tannen, V., Fundulaki, I. (eds.) SWDB 2004. LNCS, vol. 3372, pp. 140–154. Springer, Heidelberg (2005)
20. Uschfold, M., Gruninger, M.: Ontologies and Semantics for Seamless Connectivity. ACM SIGMOD Record 33(4), 58–64 (2004)
21. Wache, H., Vögele, T., Visser, U., Stuckenschmidt, H., Schuster, G., Neumann, H., Hübner, S.: Ontology-Based Integration of Information - A Survey of Existing Approaches. In: IJCAI-01 Workshop: Ontologies and Information Sharing, Seattle, WA, pp. 108–117 (2001)
22. Zhu, H., Madnick, S., Siegel, M.: Global Comparison Aggregation Services. In: 1st Workshop on E-Business, Barcelona, Spain (2002)
23. Zhu, H., Madnick, S.E: Context Interchange as a Scalable Solution to Interoperating Amongst Heterogeneous Dynamic Services. In: 3rd Workshop on eBusiness (WEB), Washington, D.C., pp. 150–161 (2004)
24. Zhu, H.: Effective Information Integration and Reutilization: Solutions to Technological Deficiency and Legal Uncertainty. In: Ph.D. Thesis. MIT, Cambridge, MA (2005)

Domain Ontologies Evolutions
to Solve Semantic Conflicts

Guilaine Talens[1], Danielle Boulanger[1], and Magali Séguran[2]

[1] MODEME, Université Jean Moulin
6 cours Albert Thomas – BP 8242
69355 Lyon cedex 08, France
{talens,db}@univ-lyon3.fr
[2] SAP Labs France, SAP Research
805, avenue du Dr. Maurice Donat
06254 Mougins Cedex
magali.seguran@sap.com

Abstract. The growth and variety of distributed information sources imply a need to exchange and/or to share information extracted from various and heterogeneous databases. The cooperation of heterogeneous information systems requires advanced architectures able to solve conflicts coming from data heterogeneity (structural and semantic heterogeneity). To resolve semantic conflicts relatively to evolutive domain ontologies following databases evolution according to the dialogue between agents, taking care of scalability issues, we propose a multi-agent system. These interaction protocols allowing ontologies evolution are currently implemented by using Java and the JADE (Java Agent DEvelopment framework) platform.

Keywords: Cooperation of heterogeneous information systems, Ontology elicitation from databases, Ontology evolution.

1   Introduction

The growth and diversity of automated information systems in organizations make the cooperation of information from heterogeneous databases [1], [2] and/or knowledge bases necessary. Every cooperative architecture has to face heterogeneity problems: technical heterogeneity (refers to various operating systems and platforms), syntactic (concerns the diversity of choices regarding data models and query languages) and application heterogeneities. This heterogeneity refers to schema, structural (like generalization/specialization conflict) and semantic heterogeneities.

In order to achieve semantic interoperability the meaning of the exchanged information must be understood across the different systems. Semantic heterogeneity is information sources dependent: semantic conflicts arise when two contexts do not use the same interpretation of the information. Semantic conflicts are classified as follows:

M. Collard (Ed.): ODBIS 2005/2006, LNCS 4623, pp. 51–67, 2007.
© Springer-Verlag Berlin Heidelberg 2007

- Synonymy conflicts (two entities semantically similar could have two different names)
- Homonymy conflicts (two entities semantically different could have similar names)
- Confounding conflicts (two attributes could be represented by different values or precisions)
- Scaling conflicts (two attributes semantically similar could be represented by different units).

Since a few years, the use of ontologies to extract implicit knowledge is a research-intensive approach to overcome semantic heterogeneity difficulties in the context of cooperation of heterogeneous information sources.

From an other point of view an agent-based solution seems well-adapted to solve semantic heterogeneity problems. In a multi-agent system, it is natural to deal with heterogeneities and conflicts: agents communicate by interaction and negotiation protocols to treat these conflicts.

In our proposal, cooperation is achieved by means of an abstract descriptive layer supporting advanced reconciliation processes and a multi-agent system. The metadata involves descriptive data objects and links constituting a knowledge base (ontology) rich enough to describe: various data models, and constraints, syntactic expressions of local available data, semantic links between local data depending on various application contexts. The knowledge base is integrated in a global project based on a multi-agent approach for heterogeneous information sources cooperation.

Because metadata are distributed in the cooperating agents we have several ontologies but as they share a common description, our approach could be qualified 'hybrid ontology approach' [3].

In first, we have briefly presented the context and the second point reminds some related works. In a third point, agent ontologies are defined. The fourth point focuses on the evolution of the agent ontologies with the interaction protocols during the semantic conflicts resolution. Finally, we conclude and expose some perspectives.

2   Related Works

Numerous projects, based on information brokering have partially dealt with the semantic conflicts solving. These systems use advanced technologies such as information mediation, agent technology or semantic representation based on ontologies, metadata or contexts [4]. For instance, whereas recent works emphasize the need for adaptive ontologies following data source evolutions [5], [6], projects often utilize global [7], [8], [9] and non scalable ontologies. The SIMS [7] model of the application domain offers a hierarchical terminological knowledge base. Each information source is related to one global ontology. INFOMASTER [8] also use single ontology approach. InfoSleuth [10] captures developments such as agent technology, domain ontologies and brokerage to support interoperation of data and services in a dynamic and open environment. InfoSleuth emphasizes on ontologies and brokers. Ontologies give a uniform and declarative description of semantic information and an ontology agent provides an overall view of ontologies. Specialized broker agents semantically match information needs in order to route requests to the relevant resources. The InfoSleuth architecture consists of a set of collaborating agents communicating by the query language KQML. Users express queries over specified ontologies via applet-based user interfaces. KIF (Knowledge Interchange Format) and SQL are used to represent queries over ontologies. Queries are routed by mediation and brokerage to specialized agents for data retrieval from distributed sources and for integration [10]. But the exact description of ontologies integration is not proposed.

In OBSERVER [11] the semantics of one information source is described by one separate ontology. It is not mentioned that the different ontologies share a common vocabulary. To compare the different ontologies, mapping rules are needed. In practice, to define inter-ontology mappings is not trivial.

SCROL [12] proposes a common ontology which specifies consensual vocabulary. The authors argue that a common ontology and the use of a semantic data model provide a complete agreement within the application domains.

COIN project [13], [14] uses a lightweight ontology coupled with powerfull algorithms to realise context mediation.

The approach chosen in PICSEL project [15] is to define an information server as a knowledge-based mediator (called domain ontology) in which the language CARIN is used as the core logical formalism to describe both the domain of applications and the contents of the relevant information sources.

Most recent projects propose an architecture of multi-agent system based on evolutive ontology in a context of e-commerce as [16]. The DASMAS project [17] presents a dialogue framework-based for resolving semantic interoperability in multi-agent systems. The approach is characterized by: several multi-agent systems with real world heterogeneous ontologies, the resolution of semantic differences at run-time through an adapted protocol and the use of WordNet lexicon in the resolution process. An ontology is associated to one multi-agent system and WordNet permits to find semantically similar concepts in the heterogeneous ontologies.

To address the problem of ontology evolution, research projects propose to build different versions of an ontology.

The problems of versioning and evolution in ontologies is significantly different with those in the relational databases [18], [19], [20]. The authors [20] define ontology versioning and evolution as 'the ability to manage ontology changes and their effects by creating and maintaining different variants of the ontology'.

In ontology evolution and versioning, two techniques exist : the first keeps track of changes in a new version or compares ontologies and computes differences or mappings between them. The second proposes automatic techniques based on heuristics comparisons to find similarities and differences between the different versions.

The OntoView system [21] helps a user to manage changes in ontologies and keeps the ontology versions. It compares the versions of ontologies and highlights the differences. It also allows the users to specify the conceptual relations between the different versions of concepts.

In [22], the researchers propose a general framework for ontology evolution that allows tools supporting different evolution tasks to share change information and leverage change information obtained by other external tools. A structural comparison of ontology versions is also proposed.

SHOE [23] does not keep track of changes from one version to another. SHOE maintains each version of the ontology as a separate web page. The ontology designer copies the original ontology file, assigns it a new version number, and adds or removes elements as needed.

In [24] through the notion of evolution strategy, the users guide the ontology evolution. They can control and customize the evolution process. [25] keeps track of different versions of an ontology and offers the possibility to allow branching and merging operations. Protegé [26] keeps track of, and records, ontology changes within the ontology itself. It also compares versions of the same ontology.

On the market, Software AG [27] emerges and has developed an XML integration solution allowing the integration of data sources as databases, XML-files and Web Services. More recently, the 'Information Integrator' [28] proposes a single and coherent view of disparate information sources by using a common ontology. This domain ontology so-called 'business ontology' reinterprets the data described in the local data-source ontologies. This reinterpretation is a way to represent complex knowledge interrelating these data. This reengineering process of the data source contents cannot be done automatically.

Scalability (the complexity of creation and maintaining the interoperation services should not increase exponentially with the number of participating local information sources) and extensibility (the ability to incorporate local information system changes without having adverse effects on other parts of the larger system) are not really treated in the case of multi-domain approaches.

Therefore, cooperative architectures with a multi-domain approach have difficulties to deal with scalability and extensibility. Thus, they do not deal with adaptative ontologies.

So, we present a proposition for semantic conflict resolution that integrates domain ontologies evolution.

3   Agent Ontologies

This work is involved in the ACSIS (Agents for the Cooperation of Secure Information System) project [29], [30], [31].

In our proposal actual information sources cooperation is based on agents interactions. Each local source is represented by one or several agents and the set of agents constitutes a multi-agent system. The scope of distributed artificial intelligence brings techniques to implement multi-agent architectures able to dynamically face the various emerging problems of information systems cooperation. The reasons for modelling a system using multiple cognitive agents are various, they range from agent cognitive capabilities to multi-agent dynamic features [32], [33]:

- Agents are autonomous, thus they can define their own internal goals and plans,
- they are able to deal with high level interactions through domain independent communication messages,
- a multi-agent architecture can dynamically evolve according to the problem to solve and even during the problem resolution,

- agents can detect changes in their environment, modify their behaviour and update their internal knowledge base describing the environment,
- they are able to cooperatively solve problems (in particular knowledge-intensive ones like semantic conflict resolution) through interactions and negotiation protocols,
- agents allow the construction of open and scalable architectures (easy addition or removal of data sources).

ACSIS architecture aims at resolving technical, syntactic, application (structural and semantic) heterogeneities that appear during the cooperative processes. Our architecture [29] comprises several levels to treat these different types of heterogeneities:

- The technical heterogeneity between information sources is performed by using a CORBA (Common Object Request Broker Architecture) middleware.
- The syntactic heterogeneity is resolved by Data Descriptive Objects (cf. paragraph 3.2) ensuring the homogenization of local data or knowledge bases.
- The structural and semantic heterogeneity is resolved during query processing by using multi-agent system and interaction protocols.

Scalable domain ontologies are used to represent the agents' knowledge corpus. Each agent owns its ontology. The agents and their ontologies are described as follows.

3.1 The Agent Model

An agent comprises several units (ontology unit constituted by Data Descriptive Objects and links between these objects), acquaintances (list of closed known agents), reasoning, communication, behaviour.

The defined multi-agent system is composed of different types of agents (see Fig. 1).

The *Wrapper Agent (WA)* ensures the participation of local data to the cooperative processes. Each WA is linked to a domain from a local database and DDOs (Data Descriptive Objects) and intra-base links form its ontology.

The *Information Agent (IA)* structures the exchange between WAs during the processing of global queries and semantic conflict resolution. Its ontology is composed of the semantics links at the global level (inter-bases links). Each IA groups WAs according to semantic characteristics. An IA accesses to at least one, and potentially many information sources, and is able to collate and manipulate information extracted from these sources in order to answer the users and other IAs.

Each IA is a multi-domain agent. Its ontology is formed by the inter-bases links.

The *Interface Agent* insures intermediation between the user (expert or user role) and the other agents:

- The User Agent manages the query, validates the results and asks the re-execution of the query if the results are not correct.
- the domain Expert Agent defines some intra-base links, chooses the database type (relational/object) and gives a representative name of the domain.

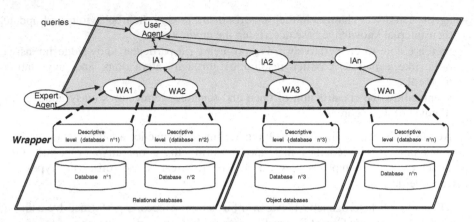

Fig. 1. The different agents

Agents exchange information by interaction protocols to solve semantic conflicts and to manage the evolution of domain ontologies.

3.2 Scalable Domain Ontologies

Models describing ontologies come from Distributed Artificial Intelligence, Knowledge representation or Databases [34]. Two different directions are envisaged:

- the first is Distributed Artificial Intelligence oriented and proposes descriptive logic with inference tools
- the second is Database-oriented and presents extended conceptual models so as to represent all the informations.

We will adopt the ontology definition in a database/knowledge sharing approach. Nevertheless, we integrate some inference rules. Ontology is an explicit, partial specification of a conceptualization [35]. A conceptualization could be a set of concepts, relations, objects and constraints defining the domain semantic model. An ontology can be defined as a specific vocabulary and relationships used to described certain aspects of reality and a set of explicit assumptions regarding the intended meaning of the words vocabulary [36].

Recently, other definitions are used in the context of oriented mediation-cooperation projects. Mena gave the following precise definition [37]:

'ontology is a description of the concepts and relationships that can exist for an agent or a community of agents. This definition is consistent with the usage of ontology as set-of-concept-definitions, but more general. And it is certainly a different sense of word than its use in philosophy. Ontology is a set of terms of interest in a particular information domain and the relationships among them'.

In our approach, the ontology of each agent contains Data Descriptive Objects (DDO) and links between these objects [29]. The DDOs contain the description of data from local information sources as well as the access primitives to this data. Local information entities (relation, relation attribute, primary key, object type, object attribute...) are described so that each information source involving the cooperation process is represented by a set of DDOs. The *relation/object* DDOs describe a class or a relation. There is no difference between relationship or entity in our modeling process, each concept is a *relation* DDO. The *attribute* DDOs include object attributes (it could be *object attribute* or *reference object attribute* that stores a pointer on an object) and *relation attributes* (it could be *primary key, foreign key* or *relation attribute*).

The **links** connect DDOs, according to schematic, structural or semantic characteristics.

Schematic Links between these DDOs are automatically extracted. The figure 2 presents the relations: *firm* (id firm, name), *office worker* (id, firstname, wage, id firm).

The *dependence links* allow connecting the attribute DDOs to a relation/object DDO.

The *reference links* allow to connect a reference DDO and a refereed DDO.

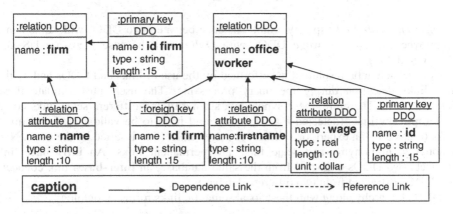

Fig. 2. Reference and dependence links between DDOs

Structural Links (generalization, specialization) are automatically extracted in the case of object approach or defined by a domain expert in the case of relational approach.

Semantic Links connect two DDOs, according to their semantic characteristics. The links are defined either by a domain expert or are automatically created during the query processing.

Synonymy Links describe a similar sense between two DDOs with different name (for example between *employee* DDO and *office worker* DDO).

Non Synonymy Links describe a different sense between two DDOs with different names.

Similarity Links describe a similar sense between two DDOs with same name.

Homonymy Links describe a different sense between two DDOs with same name (*name* DDO and *name* DDO if *name* is the attribute of *project* and *name* is the attribute of *employee* (see Fig. 3)).

Scale Links describe a same scale between DDOs which have a same unit (employee *wage* DDO and director *wage* DDO with *Dollar* unit).

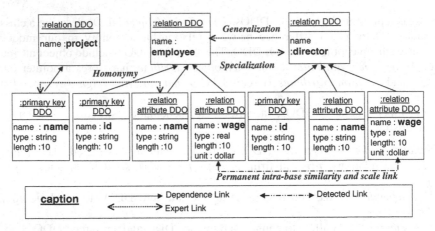

Fig. 3. Ontology example

Different Scale Links specify a unit existence between two DDOs with same name (employee and director *wage* DDOs with *Dollar* unit because there are US and Canadian dollar).

Conflict semantic resolution is performed by the use of links and DDOs and by the new links detection during the query processing. The user must validate these detected links. Therefore, these synonymy, similarity and different scale links could be **temporary** links (detected by the system and have to be validated), **permanent** links (created by an expert, or validated) or **user** links (link inserted by the user). Non synonymy, homonymy and scale links are permanent links. An **intra-base** link connects two DDOs extracted from the same database; an **inter-bases** link connects two DDOs extracted from two different databases.

DDOs hierarchy along with these local semantic links forms an ontology.

4   Interaction Protocols and Ontologies Evolutions

The interactions between agents are managed by a set of rules that forms interaction protocols dedicated to conflict resolution.

In ACSIS project, interactions reuse the FIPA protocols [38]. The conflict resolution is performed in a dynamic way during the insertion of a new information source and the global query processing. The conflicts are solved relatively to the link exploitation. The interaction protocols allow the domain ontologies to evolve with the automatic detection of new links. When the detected links are validated, a semantic inference process also allows the ontologies evolution.

In [39], an ontology is used to describe interaction protocols. Thanks to the global ontology, the agents can dynamically adapt their behavior. In ACSIS project, the interaction protocols cannot be changed because only the ontologies encapsulated in the agents evolve, not the agents. These latter transfer the informations according to predefined interaction protocols.

4.1 Insertion of a New Information Source

The registration step begins with the creation of a WA (a Wrapper Agent is created for one database) and continues with the attachment to an IA (Information Agent).

Creation Step of a WA

The DDO hierarchy with the extracted links is encapsulated in a WA. Once created, each WA can automatically detect temporary intra-base similarity links relatively equivalence based on the DDO's name (for example, *director.wage* (dollar) and *employee.wage* (dollar)). If a unit is specified in the *attribute DDOs,* some scale difference links are created. For the scale, we cannot detect equivalence with the name of the unit because wage (dollar) and wage (dollar) could not be a scale link (for example, it could be US dollar or Canadian dollar). *Temporary similarity and different scale* links are created if there are not existing homonymy and scale links.

Some *similarity* and *scale* links between *attribute DDOs* could be created in a *permanent* mode if specialization/ generalization links exist between the respective relation DDOs.

The following example (see Fig. 3) presents the relations: *project* (name), *employee* (id, name, wage), *director* (id, name, wage). The *director* relation DDO specializes *employee* relation DDO. So, there are a permanent similarity and scale link between the *wage* attribute DDO (depending of *director* relation DDO) and the *wage* attribute DDO (depending of *employee* relation DDO). The expert creates only some intra-base links which cannot be automatically created, for example the homonymy links. He also specifies the database domains.

Registration of a WA to an IA

The Registration protocol allows the registration of a WA (when a new source integrates the system) and therefore increases the WA network attached to an Information Agent. Each WA dynamically queries to be joined to the IAs that are previously created. The IA, whose domain is semantically the closest, integrates this WA into its acquaintance network (the Contract Net Protocol allows to choose the WA). The IA establishes a comparison between the network's WA so as to create temporary inter-bases similarity and different scale links (the *Fipa Query Protocol* is used).

When a new WA is recorded into an IA, the different DDOs are sent to the other WAs in order to discover new temporary inter-bases links. In our example, five similarity links are created:

– firm name DDO respectively with employee name, with director name, with project name,
– office worker wage respectively with employee wage DDO, with director wage DDO.

Two different scale links are added: office worker wage respectively with employee wage DDO, with director wage DDO.

4.2 The Global Query Processing Protocol

The global query processing protocol organizes the negotiation phases between the IAs and the WAs to resolve semantic conflicts. There are different phases in the global query processing protocol (principally based on the *Fipa Query Protocol*):

Transmission of the Query from the User Agent to IAs and WAs
Each Information Agent looks for its inter-bases semantic links and broadcasts the query to the WAs of its acquaintance network all the while taking into account its inter-bases links.

Semantic evaluation
Each WA accepts or refuses the query request relatively on knowledge of query elements by using synonymy intra-base links and homonymy links.

Links of others IAs
When the WAs of the acquaintance network don't have sufficient knowledge to answer the query, the IA asks other IAs inter-bases synonymy links to modify the concepts of the query. The modified query is send again to its connected WAs.

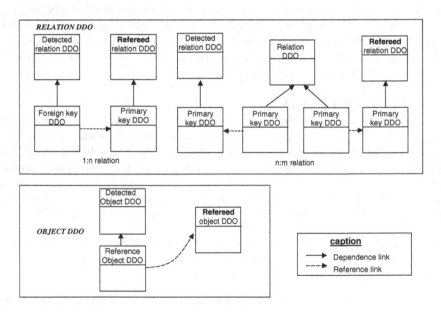

Fig. 4. Selection of the refereed DDO with reference and dependence links

Creation of New Temporary Intra-base Synonymy Links
During this semantic evaluation, each WA can create temporary intra-base synonymy through some schematic links (like the *reference links* and *dependence* links) according to the following method:

- Item 1. For each query element, if none DDO corresponds, there is a selection of the refereed DDO relatively dependence and reference links, from detected DDO (see Fig. 4).
- Item 2. If there is no attribute specified in the query, or if the specified attribute is equivalent to the attribute DDO depending of the object/relation DDO, a temporary intra-base synonymy link is created between the reference DDO and a virtual object/relation DDO (a virtual DDO is a DDO only created for the representation of this temporary link). If the attribute specified in the query matches with the attribute DDO depending of the reference DDO, a temporary intra-base similarity link is created between this attribute DDO and the attribute element of the query.

In the following example (see Fig. 5), the database contains the relations: *project* (name), *work* (id, name) and *employee* (id).

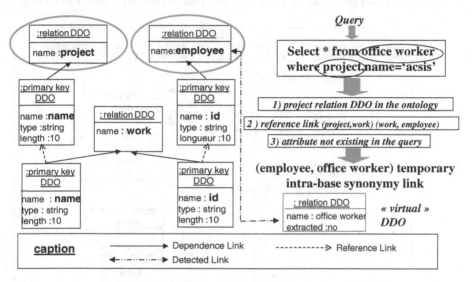

Fig. 5. Creation of a temporary intra-base synonymy link

The query is "select * from office worker where project.name='acsis'". The *office worker* DDO does not exist in the WA's ontology. Relatively to the *reference link* between *project* (existing element in the ontology) and *work* and, *work* and *employee*, the refereed *employee* DDO is selected. There is no attribute relevant *to office worker* indicated in the query (respect of item 2). Therefore, a temporary intra-base synonymy link is created between the *employee DDO* and an *office worker* virtual DDO. The WA replies with these temporary intra-base synonymy links and with the DDO names equivalent to the query elements.

Creation of New Temporary Inter-bases Synonymy Links
When the WAs send some temporary intra-base synonymy links to their IA, the IA could create some temporary inter-bases synonymy links if there is the same term in an other WA of its acquaintance network. For example, the *office worker* DDO exists in another WA. A temporary inter-bases synonymy link is created between the *office*

worker DDO and the *employee* DDO. When there is a creation of synonymy and similarity link, a corresponding link to validate is instantiated, and passed from the IA or WA to the User Agent. It allows simplifying the queries execution on the local databases. A sub-query comprises only the global query parts on which the IA has the relevant knowledge and replaces term by using temporary inter-bases synonymy links. The IAs then contact the WAs which contain knowledge in order to perform the sub-query.

Retrieving the Results

Each WA can accept or refuse (agree/refuse performative) to process the query. If it agrees, it queries its local database using temporary and permanent semantic intra-base links and structural links, retrieves data coming from local sources via DDOs and sends them to its IA (inform or failure performative).

The global query processing is presented (see Fig. 6) by using Agent UML [40].

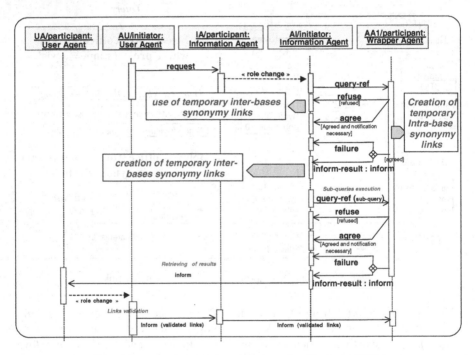

Fig. 6. Protocol for global query processing (in Agent UML)

For example, if the query is "select * from employee where employee.name='smith'", with the specialization/generalization link, the following query "select * from director where director.name='smith'" is also executed. When they retrieves the results, each WA (at the local level) and each IA (at the global level) uses intra-base or inter-bases different scale links to translate data in the expected format (if conversion functions are detected in the DDOs).

Validation of Results
Each IA restructures the responses obtained from its WAs and sends them to the user agent. At the end of the protocol, the ontologies are updated when new semantic links are discovered and after the validation of these links by the User Agent. If synonymy, similarity and different scale links are validated, they become permanent links : if they are not validated, they become non synonymy, homonymy and scale links. The User Agent can insert synonymy links if the results are not correct. Some creation of synonymy links could be performed by the WA or the IA:

– An *inter-base synonymy link (user type)* is created if the two involved terms are situated in the two different WA.
– An *intra-base synonymy link (user type)* is created if the two involved terms are situated in the same WA. An intra-base synonymy link is created using a virtual DDO as soon as a term is in a WA.

Sub-queries (WA or IA level) are re-executed in several cases (see Fig. 7):

– when intra-base or inter-bases links are not validated, the sub-queries are re-executed at the WA level or the IA level,
– when synonymy links are inserted by the user, only the modified parts of the query are re-executed towards the WA, the results being preserved at the level of each IA,
– when conversion functions are inserted by the user (they are encapsulated within the validated links towards IAs which transmit to the WAs), the corresponding sub-query must be again re-executed.

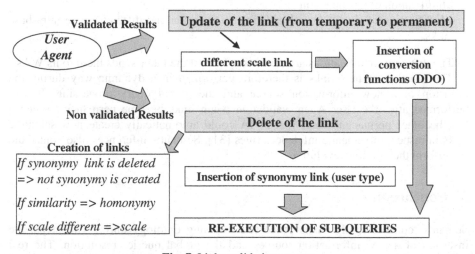

Fig. 7. Links validation process

4.3 Database Update

Different problems arise with the ontology modifications: Incompatibility of instances and incompatibility of the related applications. In ACSIS, they are managed by the database administrator in respect of the local sources autonomy.

Further, we think to use ontology versioning to capture the evolution proposed by the user as long as it is not a sound and validated evolution.

Different modifications can be performed on a database. Incompatibilities of linked ontologies are managed as follows.

	Addition	Deletion	Modification
Relation/Class	Adding of the corresponding DDO	Deletion of the DDO and updating of the concerned links	- name - attribute adding - attribute deletion
Attribute	Adding of the corresponding DDO	Deletion of the DDO and updating of the concerned links	- name - type (modification of the DDO) - unit

- Addition :
  The creation of similarity and different scale intra-base links is processed as for the insertion of a new database as previously explained. The new DDOs are compared with the other DDOs in order to create new links.
- Deletion :
  The intra-base links are deleted but not the inter-bases links because they constitute global knowledge.
- Modification of attribute, relation or class name:
  Modification of the concerned DDO, creation of a virtual DDO in order to store the old name and creation of a synonymy link between the two DDOs.
- Modification of attribute unit :
  Modification of the DDO and updating of the scale and different scale intra-base links.

The different modifications are sent to the IA and the latter sends them to its WAs.

The creation of new links is therefore performed in a dynamic way during the insertion of a new information source and the global query processing. It also performed after the User Agent validation when links become permanent. When a link becomes permanent, each WA or IA could automatically create new semantic links in respect of semantic inferences rules [31]. Semantic inferences also contribute to perform the ontology evolution.

5   Conclusion

Semantic conflict resolution is processed by using ontology during two steps: the insertion of a new information sources and the global queries resolution. The real dialogue between agents managed by a protocol, enables agents' ontologies to evolve. The scalability of the system comes from the new link detection (scalable domain ontology) and the ability of following the evolution of local databases (relatively to the DDOs level). The cooperative architecture with the interaction protocols is implemented by using Java and the JADE platform (Java Agent DEvelopment framework) [41][42]. JADE is a software framework to develop agent-based applications in compliance with the FIPA specifications for interoperable intelligent multi-agent systems and provides a library of FIPA interaction protocols ready to be used. JADE provides a support for content language and ontologies allowing the developers manipulating information within their agents as Java objects without the need of any extra work. The JADE support performs the conversion between the information represented as a string or a sequence of bytes at ACL Message level and Information represented as Java objects (easy to manipulate) at agent level. In our platform, this support has been useful to pass links and queries objects. Currently the prototype runs. We have implemented the main protocols and processed some queries. We have proposed a solution based on an extended conceptual model integrating some principles coming from Distributed Artificial Intelligence like interaction protocols between agents and inference rules on the detected links. It is a mixed approach combining advantage from descriptive logics and an extended conceptual model. In our future works, we wish to continue to integrate tools of reasoning in the model of evolutive ontologies proposed in this article.

The concept of version must be developed on the ontology to capture the modifications performed by the user. The ontology must be not directly modified as long as the modifications have not been completely validated. The user's modification becomes public after its validation by a super user or an administrator. Our ontology versions will keep track of the different modifications (add, update, delete) in order to better follow the evolution and to perform the impacts on the other ontologies after the version validation.

References

1. Bouguettaya, A., Benatallah, B., Elmagarmid, A.K.: Multidatabase Systems: Past and Present. In: Elmagarmid, A.K., Rusinkiewicz, M., Sheth, A. (eds.) Distributed and Heterogeneous Database Systems. Morgan Kauffmann, San Francisco (1998)
2. Fankhauser, P., Gardarin, G., Lopez, M., Muñoz, J., Tomasic, A.: Experiences in Federated Data-bases From IRO-DB to MIRO-Web. In: 24th VLDB'98, New-York, USA, pp. 655–658 (1998)
3. Wache, H., Vogele, T., Visser, U., Stuckenschmidt, H., Schuster, G., Neumann, H., Hubner, S.: Ontology-Based Integration - a survey of Existing Approaches. In: IJCAI'01 Workshop: Ontologies and Information Sharing, pp. 108–117 (2001)
4. Sheth, A.: Changing Focus on Interoperability in Information Systems: from System, Syntax, Structure to Semantics. In: Interoperating Geographic Information Systems. Kluwer Academic Publishers, Boston, MA (1999)
5. Kahng, J., Mac Leod, D.: Dynamic Classificational Ontologies. In: Arbid, M.A., Grethe, J. (eds.) Computing the Brain : A Guide to Neuroinformatics. Academic Press, San Diego (2000)
6. Gal, A.: Semantic Interoperability in Information Services. Experiencing with CoopWARE. ACM Sigmod record 28(1) (1999)
7. Arens, Y., Chee, C.Y., Hsu, C., Knoblock, C.A.: Retrieving and Integrating Data from Multiple Information Sources. IJCIS 2(2), 127–157 (1993)
8. Genesereth, M.R., Keller, A.M., Duschka, O.M.: Infomaster: an Information Integration. System. In: Proceedings of the ACM SIGMOD Conference (1997)
9. Aparicio, A.S., Farias, O.L.M., dos Santos, N.: Applying Ontologies in the Integration of Heterogeneous Relational Databases. In: Australian Ontology Workshop, AOW'2005, Sydney, Australia (2005)

10. Nodine, M., ali.: Active Information Gathering in InfoSleuth. IJCIS 9(1-2), 3–28 (2000)
11. Mena, E., Illarramendi, A., Kashyap, V., Shet, A.: Observer: an approach for query processing in global information systems based on interoperation across pre-existing ontologies. Int'l Journal Distributed and Parallel Databases 8(2), 223–271 (2000)
12. Ram, S., Park, J.: Semantic Conflict Resolution Ontology (SCROL): An Ontology for detecting and resolving data- and schema-level semantic conflicts. IEEE Transactions on knowledge and data engineering 16(2), 189–202 (2004)
13. Goh, C.H.: Representing and Reasoning about Semantic Conflicts in Heterogeneous Information Sources. PhD. MIT, Cambridge, MA (1997)
14. Zhu, H., Madnick, S.: Structured contexts with lightweight ontology. In: VLDB Workshop on Ontologies-based techniques for DataBases and Information Systems, Korea (2006)
15. Reynaud, C., Safar, B.: Representation of ontoloies for Information Integration. In: Gómez-Pérez, A., Benjamins, V.R. (eds.) EKAW 2002. LNCS (LNAI), vol. 2473, Springer, Heidelberg (2002)
16. Rosaci, D.: A Model of Agent Ontologies for B2C E-Commerce. In: Proceedings of the International Conference on Enterprise Information Systems (ICEIS 2004), Porto, Portugal, pp. 3–9 (2004)
17. Orgun, B., Dras, M., Nayak, A.: DASMAS – Dialogue based Automation of Semantic Interoperability in Multi Agent Systems. In: Australian Ontology Workshop, AOW'2005, Sydney, Australia (2005)
18. Bounif, H.: Predictive Approach for Database Schema Evolution. In: Ma, Z.M. (ed.) Intelligent Databases. Idea Group Publishing, USA (2006)
19. Bounif, H., Pottinger, R.: Schema Repository for Database Schema Evolution. In: Bressan, S., Küng, J., Wagner, R. (eds.) DEXA 2006. LNCS, vol. 4080, pp. 647–651. Springer, Heidelberg (2006)
20. Noy, N.F., Klein, M.: Ontology Evolution: Not the same as Schema Evolution. Knowledge and Information Systems 5 (2003)
21. Klein, M., Kiryakov, A., Ognyanov, D., Fensel, D.: Ontology versioning and change detection on the web. In: Gómez-Pérez, A., Benjamins, V.R. (eds.) EKAW 2002. LNCS (LNAI), vol. 2473. Springer, Heidelberg (2002)
22. Klein, M., Noy, N.F.: A component based framework for ontology evolution. In: Workshop on Ontologies and Distributed Systems, IJCAI'03, Mexico (2003)
23. Heflin, J., Hendler, J.: Dynamic Ontologies on the Web. In: Proceedings of the 17th national conference on Artificial Intelligence, AAAI 2000, pp. 443–449. AAAI/MIT Press, Menlo Park, CA (2000)
24. Stojanovic, L., et al.: User-driven Ontology Evolution Management. In: Proceedings of the 13th International Conference on Knowledge Engineering and Knowledge Management, Ontologies and the semantic web (2002)
25. Auer, S., Herre, H.: A Versioning and Evolution Framework for RDF Knowledge Bases. In: Proceedings of Ershov Memorial Conference (2006)
26. Liang, Y., Alani, H., Shadbolt, N.R.: Ontology change management in Protégé. In: Proceedings of Advanced Knowledge Technologies Doctoral Colloquim, United Kingdom (2005)
27. Software AG: http://www.softwareag.com/fr/
28. Angele, J., Gesmann, M.: Semantic Information Integration with Software AGs Information Integrator. In: Second International Conference on Rules and Rule markup languages for the Semantic Web, Athens, Georgia, USA (2006)
29. Boulanger, D., Dubois, G.: An Object Approach for Information System Cooperation. Information Systems 23(6), 383–399 (1998)

30. Couturier, V., Séguran, M.: Patterns and Components to Capitalise and Reuse a Cooperative Information System Architecture. In: Int'l Conf on Enterprise Information System Architecture ICEIS 2003, Angers, April 23-26, pp. 225–231 (2003)
31. Séguran, M.: Résolution des conflits sémantiques dans les systèmes d'information coopératifs. PhD thesis, Université Jean Moulin, Lyon, France (2003)
32. Papazoglou, M., Laufmann, S., Sellis, T.: An Organizational Framework for Cooperating Intelligent Information Systems. IJCIS 1(1) (1992)
33. Klusch, M.: Intelligent Agent Technology for the Internet: A Survey. Journal on Data and Knowledge Engineering. In: Fensel, D. (ed.) Special Issue on Intelligent Information Integration, vol. 36(3), Elsevier Science (2001)
34. Cullot, N., ali.: Ontologies: A contribution to the DL/DB debate. In: Proceedings of the 1rst Int'l Workshop on Semantic Web and Database (SWDB'2003) co-located VLDB'2003, Germany, pp. 109–130 (2003)
35. Gruber, T.: The Role of a Common Ontology in Achieving Sharable, Reusable Knowledge Bases. In: Proceedings of the 2nd International Conference on Principles of Knowledge Representation and Reasoning, pp. 601–602. Cambridge University Press, Cambridge (1991)
36. Guarino, N.: Formal Ontology and Information Systems. In: Proceedings of the 1st International Conference on Formal Ontology in Information Systems (FOIS'98), Torino, pp. 3–15 (1998)
37. Mena, E., Illarramendi, A.: Ontology-based Query Processing for Global Information Systems. Kluwer Academic Publishers, Boston, MA (2001)
38. Fipa: http://www.fipa.org
39. Toivonen, S., Helin, H.: Representing Interaction Protocols in DAML. In: van Elst, L., Dignum, V., Abecker, A. (eds.) AMKM 2003. LNCS (LNAI), vol. 2926, pp. 310–321. Springer, Heidelberg (2004)
40. Odell, J., Parunak, H., Bauer, B.: Extending UML for Agents. In: Wagner, G., Lesperance, Y., Yu, E. (eds.) Proceedings of Agent-Oriented Information Systems Workshop at the 17 th National conference on Artificial Intelligence. Icue Publishing, Austin, Texas (2000)
41. Bellifemine, F.: Jade and beyonds. Presentation at AgentCities Information Day 1, Lausanne (2002)
42. Jade: http://sharon.cselt.it/projects/jade

Requirements Ontology and Multi-representation Strategy for Database Schema Evolution

Hassina Bounif, Stefano Spaccapietra, and Rachel Pottinger

Database Laboratory, EPFL, School of Computer and Communication Science
Lausanne, Switzerland
Data Management and Mining Laboratory, University of British Columbia
Vancouver, Canada
hassina.bounif@epfl.ch,
stefano.spaccapietra@epfl.ch, rap@cs.ubc.ca

Abstract. With the emergence of enterprise-wide information systems, ontologies have become by definition a valuable aid for efficient database schema modeling and integration, in addition to their use in other disciplines such as the semantic web and natural language processing. This paper presents another important utilization of ontologies in database schemas: schema evolution. Specifically, our research concentrates on a new three-layered approach for schema evolution. These three layers are 1) a schema repository, 2) a domain ontology called a *requirements ontology*, and 3) a multi-representation strategy to enable powerful change management. This a priori approach for schema evolution, in contrast with existing a posteriori solutions, can be employed for any data model and for both 1) design from scratch and evolution and 2) redesign and evolution of the database. The paper focuses on the two main foundations of this approach, the requirements ontology and the multi-representation strategy which is based on a stamping mechanism.

Keywords: Requirements ontology, multi-representation strategy, Schema Evolution.

1 Introduction

With the emergence of enterprise-wide information systems, the number of ontologies in semantic-driven data access and processing is increasing. For example, ontologies are crucial in semantic web and natural language processing. In addition to that, ontologies have become a valuable aid for efficient database schemas modeling and integration – they provide richer semantics than studying the schemas alone. This work investigates another area in which ontologies have a colossal potential of utilization and which is related to information systems: database schema evolution. Database schema evolution has an active research agenda due to its importance, cost to users, and the complexity of the problem. Many solutions have been proposed and much progress has been made in data structures, rules, constraints, schemata models and meta-models. We build on this work and advocate a novel approach for schema evolution: we predict potential changes, and integrate them into the schema for future

M. Collard (Ed.): ODBIS 2005/2006, LNCS 4623, pp. 68–84, 2007.

use. Since predicting the exact changes that *will* occur over time is impossible, we detect the changes that *are plausible to be* carried out on a schema and are important for the database users. Our intent is to move one step towards developing multi-disciplinary and a priori approaches for database schema evolution, in contrast with existing a posteriori solutions that track changes instead of planning for them.

Our approach relies on the use of: 1) a schema repository that stores and provides to the system a set of relevant schemas and their relative versions, if any. In our case, the repository contains approximately 4000 schemas, 2) a requirements ontology that contains the changes that are plausible to be carried out on a database schema and are important for the database users and 3) a multi-representation strategy to aid powerful change management.

1.1 Problem Description

Having understood the overall motivation of schema evolution and our predictive approach, we are now ready to explain schema evolution in more detail. Intuitively, schema evolution means the ability of a schema to undergo changes over time without any loss of the extant data. However, besides managing the changes to the schema, applications and data linked to it need to be adapted as well. Changes to the schema are divided into three categories depending on their impact on the schema [1]:

1- Additive   : additional semantic knowledge needs to be designed on the schema
2- Subtractive: semantic knowledge needs to be removed from the schema
3-Descriptive: the same semantic knowledge needs to be designed on the schema in a different manner.

In addition to the categories of changes that could occur on the schema over time, we need to consider the general problem of database schema evolution from two different sides, depending on the kind of solution we choose: 1) From the a posteriori solution perspective, 2) From the a priori solution perspective

1) From the a posteriori solution perspective
Historically, from this perspective, to resolve the schema evolution problem, one should take into consideration two major criteria, which are respectively [2]: a) the semantics of change, i.e. the understanding of the change that has taken place because of several reasons such as the new perceptions of the real world over time and technology development and performance strategies and b) the propagation of this change on the schema immediately or at a deferred time fixed by the database administrator. There is a posterior order in which the change must be received after by the schema and its components. Schema evolution is resolved either by versioning the original schema, by modifying it using restricted evolution primitives, by adopting views on the top of it or by refining it by accommodating the exceptional information in the database [3]. All these solutions react to changes that could occur on the schema. However, they are insufficient solutions, especially when the schema is facing complex changes. For instance, the modification approach simply modifies the schema to adhere to the new requirements. This changing of the schema without saving past information may lead to a loss of data. The versioning approach replicates the schema to save both the old and the new version. This replication avoids data loss;

however, it creates complex navigation through the different generated versions and slows down the DBMS (Database Management System). The combination solution – a solution that incorporates both existing approaches (e.g. the work presented in [4]) – avoids the above problems. Unfortunately, it also is characterized by the complexity and the onerous mechanisms to be executed. Hence, a new approach must be used; the a priori solution.

2) From a priori solution perspective

To resolve the problem of schema evolution from this perspective, one must clearly take into account these imperative criteria:

- Understand the current database structure and content
- Identify the dependencies among the current database schema, data and applications because the impact of one element on another needs to be known and accounted for before making changes on the database
- Detect potential changes that are plausible to occur on the schema
- Understand the potential future changes and new applications and identify their impacts on the current schema
- Consider the two possible cases, related to the database, that are respectively: 1) the case in which the initial database schema is not created yet and 2) the case in which the initial schema has already been created; however, it needs to be redesigned.

Compared to the previous perspective, in the a priori solution, the order of applicability of the changes has been modified. The changes are incorporated before they really occur. There is what is called an a priori order in which the potential change must be received before by the schema and its components.

1.2 Contribution and Outline of the Paper

The contributions of this paper are as follows:

1. Presentation of the predictive approach for database schema evolution, including the characteristics and the differences with other existing approaches for schema evolution
2. Presentation of the requirements ontology, including its role, construction and structure
3. Presentation of the multi-representation strategy with the two defined mechanisms views and stamping
4. Presentation of examples showing how the predictive approach works and outlining the role of both the requirements ontology and the multi-representation strategy.

The paper comprises five main sections. Section 2 presents the articulation of the predictive approach. Section 3 presents 1) the role of the requirements ontology in the predictive approach for evolution and 2) the structure and how it is built from the schema repository. Section 4 describes the multi-representation strategy and how it is used for schema evolution. Section 5 presents a motivating example to demonstrate the feasibility of the proposed approach. Section 6 is a conclusion and a summary of the important points dealt with in this paper and introduces perspectives on the future work.

2 Predictive Approach for Schema Evolution

The predictive approach for schema evolution is an innovative approach for schema evolution. In this section, we consider some of the specific characteristics that justify the decision of the selection of such approach. We begin by listing them, and then consider each one in more depth in turn:

- A priori solution (a)
- Predictive analytic solution (b)
- Proactive schema solution (c)
- Three different stages solution (d)
- Data modeling methodology independent solution (e)
- Collecting data solution (f)

a) A priori Approach
In contrast with existing posterior solutions for evolution such as modification or versioning approaches that support the evolution at evolution time, the *Predictive Approach* prepares the database schema for future use before the changes occur. The basic motivations that influence our choice of a methodology that plans in advance for evolution are: 1) the problem of schema evolution is better understood now because researchers have already provided an overview of its causes and consequences, therefore it is now time to turn towards complex and multi-disciplinary approaches 2) the posteriori approaches have not been sufficient solutions for schema evolution even if they are considered to be standard solutions and finally 3) the a priori approach is absolutely the best alternative: the key to evolution problem lies in thinking of the evolution from the beginning of the lifecycle of the database.

b) Predictive analytic solution
A predictive solution generally refers to data mining techniques such as classification to predict the value of a particular attribute based on the value of other attributes. The attribute to be predicted is called the dependent variable while the attributes used for making prediction are called the independent variables [5]. Our predictive solution 1) uses data-mining techniques such as Classification Based on Association Rules, and 2) in particular, it explicitly includes a requirement analysis phase. In the requirements analysis phase, besides assessing the current user requirements via the database user's feedback and comments, additional requirements called *potential future requirements* are investigated using the current requirements of several databases. These new requirements, representing potential future needs that might emerge during the lifecycle of the database in the future are inspected inside a schema repository. In this case, the current requirements are representing the independent variables while the future requirements are the dependent variables.

c) Proactive schema solution
Our solution takes actions to handle changes before the evolution of the database schema. In other words, this approach generates a scalable database schema called the *predicted schema* at design time that contains three different layers which are respectively: 1) Operational Layer, 2) Existing but not Operational Layer, 3) Not Existing but Planned Layer. In these three layers, the schema potential structural changes are hold at the present time for its use in the evolution time.

d) Three different stages solution
The approach holds one additional stage which is novel in database modeling design; in contrast existing approaches enclose just two stages: (1) design time and (2) evolution time. The additional third stage of the predictive approach, the *before design time stage*, is an important stage. It paves the way for the design time stage by conducting the preparation of the accurate data for the schema evolution from the schema repository.

e) Data modeling methodology independent solution
Because of the diversity of the data models used to represent a database schema, we have chosen to develop an approach that can be adopted by any modeling methodology.

f) Collecting data solution
Our solution uses the direct collection of information from different external sources and a consultation of schemas of existing databases.

There are multiple advantages of this approach. Indeed, it contributes significantly in the ability of the database schema to 1) accommodate the future changes, and 2) facilitate the work of designers and help them save time and money on the evolution of their databases. Consequently, all these qualities have a positive impact on both database users and the organisms that employ such pre-emptive approaches.

3   Requirements Ontology for Schema Evolution

The requirements ontology is a domain ontology in which requirements are expressed with concepts (terms), relationships and constraints. It allows the system to relate the current schema to possible future needs. For example, if a database designer needs to create a database for meetings, the requirements ontology associated to this database contains concepts, relationships and constraints related to meeting domain such as *MEETING, PARTICIPANT, ROOM* and *AGENDA* concepts and *IS, HAS* relationship types and so on. This is illustrated in figure 1. The requirements ontology gains its insights into the possible future needs of the schema through various methods; its construction is described further in Section 3.2.
    The requirements ontology looks like a global entity relationship model; however, it is richer than an entity relationship model because 1) it contains more semantics related to a specific domain. 2) the instances of the requirements ontology are divided into two categories: in addition to the instances representing the current requirements, the database designer needs to choose the concepts that might correspond to potential future requirements. Consequently, several design suggestions about the entities with their relationships are taken from the requirements ontology and are provided to the database designers.

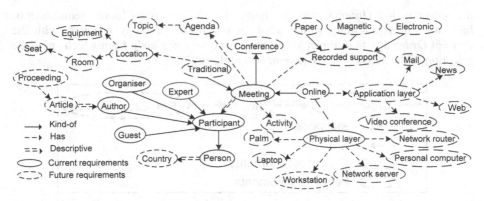

Fig. 1. Presentation of a part of requirements ontology of meeting domain

Since the system is designed to be flexible enough for many situations, and it is impossible to predict with 100% accuracy which requirements will be desired, the system includes three strategies to the database designers for the selection of those requirements ontology concepts and their corresponding relationships. These strategies are:

1) Blind selection: all the concepts of the requirements ontology belonging to future requirements are selected without exception.

2) Case based selection: This selection mechanism allows the inclusion of concepts that are particularly likely to be needed in the future. In particular, the concepts that satisfy one of the following cases are selected. This is a way to find out the important concepts that have already pre-established links among them
Case 2.a: a concept belonging to future requirements which is situated between two concepts of current requirements. This is illustrated in figure 2.

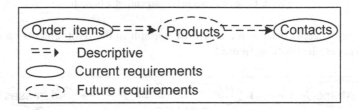

Fig. 2. Case of future concept between current concepts

Case 2.b: a concept that is a final node (part i) or belongs to the end of a branch in the requirements ontology (part ii) is selected. This is illustrated in figure 3 and 4.

- (i) A final node
A final node is a concept in the requirements ontology which has only one relationship with another concept of the requirements ontology. For example in figure 3,

the concept *Ref_Order_Status*, belonging to the category future requirements, has only one relationship in the whole requirements ontology which is with the concept *Order* that is its direct ancestor. An ancestor is a node from which starts the selection of the nodes of the requirements ontology.

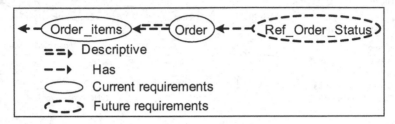

Fig. 3. Case of a concept as a final node

- (ii) An end of a branch
A branch is a sequence of concepts linked together with one or several links however one concept of this succession has only one relationship with another concept of the sequence in the whole requirements ontology. This is illustrated in figure 4 in which the concept *Product_description* is a concept of the sequence that has only one relationship with the concept *Product*.

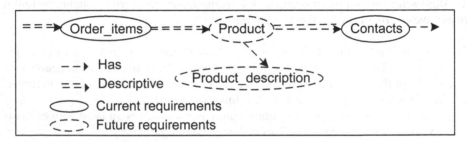

Fig. 4. Case of concepts as an end of a branch

Case 2.c: the concepts that form a clique of a graph in the requirements ontology are selected. This is illustrated in figure 5.

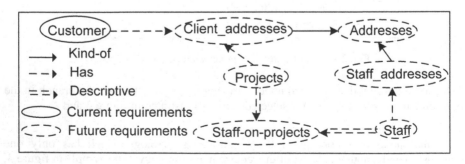

Fig. 5. Case of a clique graph

3) Change perspective selection: the concepts are selected according to their *change perspectives*. A change perspective is a special graph that shows the potential changes of each concept belonging to the ontology. It is built using several data mining techniques such as classical association rules and classification based on association rules[5]. The requirements ontology contains three different types of change perspectives with specific roles which are respectively: informative, descriptive and predictive.

To illustrate this point, we consider the following example that represents the modelling of a simple case of scientific meeting in which the requirement is to determine the people participating to a conference. At the ontological level, for the concept "Meeting", the change perspectives, illustrated in figure 6, show the potential changes related to it and the other concepts that might be implied at the evolution time.

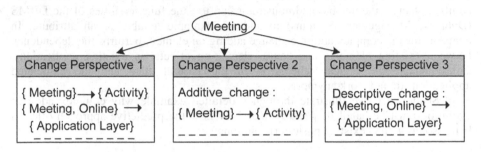

Fig. 6. Change perspectives for the concept meeting

3.1 Requirements Ontology Role

There are two ways in which the requirements ontology is used in the predictive approach for evolution. These two primary functions are 1) design and evolution and 2) redesign and evolution.

1) Design and evolution
In case the initial database schema is not created yet, the ontology fulfils several tasks, as presented in [6] and [7]: it generates a design "from" scratch using the defined terms and relationships as a representative model of the domain. It suggests possible missing entities and relationships in the case just a part or selected parts of it is/are considered by the database designer. The requirements ontology offers additional features; it includes terms, relationships and constraints that might represent potential future requirements and identifies in advance their dependencies with terms and relationships representing current requirements. Consequently, it facilitates the work of database designer when changes should be made on the schema.

2) Redesign and evolution
In case the initial schema has already been created and now needs to be redesigned, then the ontology fulfils other important tasks as presented in [6] and [7]. For

example, it is used to check for missing entities or relationships or inconsistencies in an existing or partial design because the data model produced in the redesign process, called a reverse engineered (RE) data model [8], cannot be considered as a conceptual schema. The RE model converts all the logical schema tables to entities without making distinction between data tables and the other tables of the schema whose function is to join tables. This model is not a logical schema because some important schema information is lost during the conversion process, such as in the case of foreign keys.

In the following, we portray the three categories of changes presented previously, which are 1) the additive evolution, 2) the subtractive evolution and 3) the descriptive evolution and how the requirements ontology proceeds in each case.

1) Additive Evolution

There are two types of additive changes: simple and complex. For the simple additive change, the database administrator can use the functionalities of the DBMS (Database Management Systems) to add for example a table or an attribute. In contrast, for the complex additive change adding an element perturbs the dependency between existing elements and causes damaging effects on existing applications. Consequently, the logical schema is in inconsistent state and the associated applications do not work anymore.

In Section 5.1, we illustrate through a detailed example why complex additive evolution must be handled specially and show how the predictive approach offers a better solution than existing posteriori solutions.

2) Subtractive Evolution

Subtractive evolution occurs when elements in the schema are no longer required. However, deleting an element on existing schema is not always obvious, leading to two types of subtractive changes: simple and complex. For the simple subtractive change, the database administrator can use the functionalities of the DBMS (Database Management Systems) to delete the no longer required elements. Whereas for the complex subtractive evolution, the DBMS does not offer any functions for it and the changes have direct and critical consequences on the schema and applications.

In Section 5.2, we illustrate through a detailed example why complex subtractive evolution must be handled specially and show how the predictive approach offers a better solution than existing posteriori solutions.

3) Descriptive Evolution

Descriptive evolution is made for convenience or efficiency. It is the hardest to handle in traditional database systems because it implies more than one risky modification operation on the schema. The consequences of the changes on the schema are also critical, such as data loss.

In Section 5.3, we illustrate through an example why complex descriptive evolution must be handled specially and show how the predictive approach offers a better solution than existing posteriori solutions. The lack of space in this paper does not allow us to explain in detail the example.

3.2 Requirements Ontology Construction

The requirements ontology is developed using both a schema repository in which the main concepts are extracted and WordNet ontology [9] for extracting their corresponding synonyms and antonyms. The requirements ontology consists of two kinds of partitions, the ones representing current requirements called Current sub-domains and the ones corresponding to potential future requirements called Future sub-domains.

The process of the requirements ontology creation is iterative and complex some how compared to existing approaches. It consists on four main phases: *knowledge acquisition, Data mining and informal conceptualisation, Evaluation for Refinement or Revision* and *Formal Conceptualization*

1 -Knowledge acquisition and pre-processing: consists of schemas collection and preparation

2 -Data mining algorithms and informal conceptualization: in which concepts and relationships are extracted from schema data sets repository in an unsupervised way and used as output for the informal conceptualization of the ontology from scratch.

3 -Evaluation for Refinement or Revision: means to test the validity of the concepts belonging to the taxonomy and to decide to keep or reject them using qualitative and quantitative methods.

4 -Formal Conceptualization: consists in building formally the requirements ontology using OWL and description logic.

These phases are not very developed in this paper because they necessitate a considerable space.

The schema repository contains many different schemas that model a specific domain. These schemas and their related versions may be of different types, such as ER, relational, object and object-relational schemas. The XML databases can be included as well as the ontological schemas expressed in OWL technology [10]. The schema repository has a dual role in building the requirements ontology [11]: (1) the repository serves in the data-mining process to identify and analyze trends on different kinds of schemas collected. (2) The repository contains selected concepts and relationships to be included in the requirements ontology.

3.3 Requirements Ontology Structure

The structure of this ontology includes: a) Concepts, b) Relationships, c) constraints d) Current versus Future Labels, and described in more detail below:

a) Concepts (Terms) Description:
Each term has one or several attributes with one or several values and one or several synonyms and antonyms.

b) Relationships Description
Relations are between two concepts. There are six kinds of relations: (1) hierarchic – identified by the label "kind-of", which expresses the specialization of one concept

regarding another and inherits attributes from this super concept; (2) composition – identified by the label "has", which expresses that a concept is a part of another concept; (3) descriptive – when it is possible to define several types of relations and is identified by a verb form; (4) reflexive – allows self-loops in which an arc whose endpoints are the same concept.

We consider the previous example of meeting domain to show some relationships among concepts: kind-of (meeting, conference) is a hierarchic relationship, has (meeting, utterances) is a composition relationship, lives (Person, Country), originates (Person, Country) and represents (Person, Country) are descriptive relationships and finally invites (Person, Person) is a reflexive relationship.

c) Constraints
Similar to the work presented in [6] and [7], we use four types of constraints which are respectively: 1) pre-requisite constraint, 2) mutually inclusive constraint, 3) mutual exclusive constraint and 4) temporal constraint.

d) Current versus future labels
The requirements ontology is a labeled graph: special labels are added and exploited in order to indicate whether a concept, respectively a relationship belongs to current or future requirements. A concept respectively, a relationship belongs to either current requirements or future requirements but not to both at the same time. This is main structure characteristic that distinguishes the requirements ontology from the remaining domain ontologies.

e) Change perspectives

4   Multi-representation Strategy for the Predictive Approach

In the predictive approach, the predicted schema is semi-automatically generated from the requirements ontology. At the conceptual level, the predicted schema is represented either 1) with the multi-representation strategy or 2) without the representation strategy. In this paper, we stress the use of the multi-representation strategy as follows:

4.1   Definition of the Multi-representation Strategy

The multi-representation strategy is well-known in the object-modeling field, as well as in the spatial databases. In [12], the multi-representation strategy based on stamping in geographic databases is presented. On the other hand, in the object modeling, the multi-representation is called semantic object views. It allows to make the object visible for certain applications and to hide it to others using the views mechanism. In this work, we focus on the multi-presentation based on stamping.

4.2   The Predicted Schema at the Conceptual Level

This strategy consists in using stamps at the conceptual level in order to have different representations for the modeling of the same universe of discourse i.e. the modeling of the same real-world. A stamp S is defined as a vector S=<s1, s2, Sn> where each s¡ represents the ¡ representation of the real-world. For example, in the following simple example, we have defined a stamp S =<S1, S2> in which, according to the element S1 of the stamp S, the conceptual schema contains the entities E1, E1' and the relationships A1'. However, according to the element S2 of the stamp S, the conceptual schema contains the entities E1 and E2 and one relationship A1. This is illustrated in figure 7.

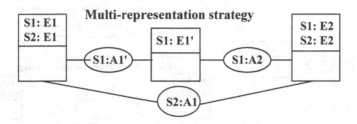

Fig. 7. A Simple Example using Multi-Representation Based on Stamping

The stamping mechanism is not a simple mechanism as it may appear. For example, in the case of successive evolutions on the database schema, the stamp components and the constraints on the stamps should be studied carefully in order to avoid any potential contradiction among them.

5   Motivating Examples

In this section, we present examples of schema changes to illustrate how the predictive approach for evolution discussed in this paper works. The examples portray the three categories of changes presented previously, which are 1) the additive evolution, 2) the subtractive evolution and 3) the descriptive evolution.

5.1   Additive Evolution

A case of complex additive change is illustrated in the side 1 of the figure 8 in which the addition of the entity E'1 creates problems for existing applications. At the time **T= t0**, we have a schema with two entities **E1** and **E2** and an association between them **A1** as presented in figure 8. At the time **T=t1**, the evolution time, a schema has been modified and complex additive changes occur: an Entity **E'1** and two associations **A'1** and **A2** are added. The association **A1** between the entities **E1** and **E2** is consequently deleted to avoid a redundancy which is itself a problem and information on schema is lost. The way to resolve such a problem with the predictive consists in:

1 - At the ontological level: the database designer examines whether the requirements ontology reveals the existence of concepts/relationships that belong to the category of future requirements and represent potential simple and complex additive changes.

2- At the conceptual level, the database designer incorporates these concepts/ relationships using the multi- representation strategy based on stamping mechanism. The resulted conceptual schema represents consequently two universes of discourse (real-world). This is illustrated in the side 2 of the figure 8.

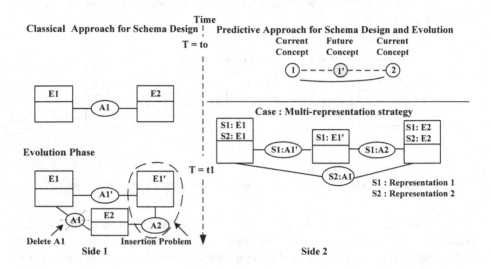

Fig. 8. Additive Evolution on an Example with both Classical and Predictive approaches

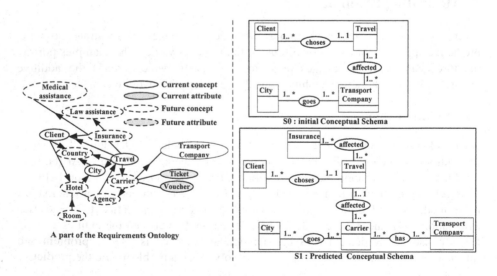

Fig. 9. An example of travel with both classical and predictive approaches

A case of complex and simple additive changes on the schema is illustrated in figure 9 where we consider the example that represents the modeling of a simple case of travel, in which the requirement is to determine the clients traveling around the world. In a classical design approach, the initial conceptual schema S0 contains four entities which are *Client, Travel, City* and *Transport Company*. However, in the predictive approach, the schema S1 that has been proposed by the requirements ontology contains six entities. The two additional entities *Insurance* and *Carrier* represent two potential future changes on the schema that belong to simple and complex additive changes respectively.

5.2 Subtractive Evolution

A case of complex subtractive change is illustrated in the side 1 of the figure 10 in which the deletion of the entity E2 creates problems for the existing applications that need such entity. The whole process to resolve such problem is illustrated in the side 2 of the figure 10.

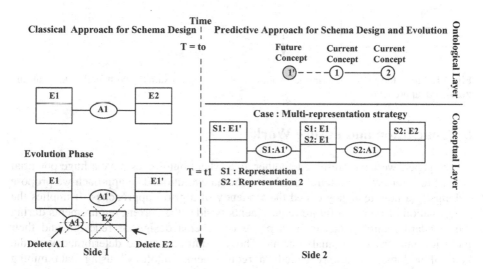

Fig. 10. Presentation of subtractive evolution on a simple example with both Classical and Predictive approaches

5.3 Descriptive Evolution

This is illustrated in the side 1 of the figure 11. Similarly to the previous, we follow the same steps for the resolution of this problem according to the predictive approach. The whole process is illustrated in the side 2 of the figure 11.

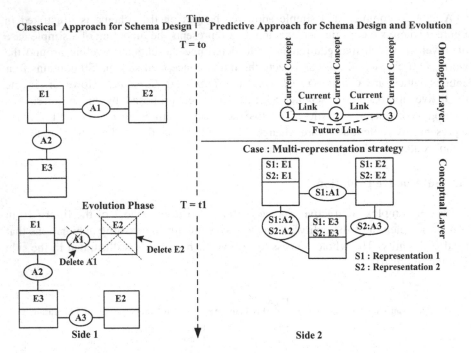

Fig. 11. Presentation of Descriptive evolution on a simple example with both Classical and Predictive approaches

6   Conclusion and Future Work

In this paper, we have presented another area where ontologies have a huge potential benefit to information systems: database schema evolution. The approach we propose belongs to a new tendency called the tendency of a priori approaches. It implies the investigation of potential future requirements besides the current requirements during the standard requirements analysis phase of schema design or redesign and their inclusion into the conceptual schema. Those requirements are determined with the help of a domain ontology called "a requirements ontology" using data mining techniques and schema repository. The advantages of this approach include: 1) new perspectives in the way requirements are inspected and integrated into the schema, 2) two categories of database designers were taken into consideration, the category of those who design a schema from scratch and the category of those who redesign the schema from existing schemas using reverse engineering and dependency graphs, 3) the reinforcement of the conceptual schemas, 4) and finally the compatibility of the approach with any data model.

Prediction in schema evolution means to envision the potential changes that could occur over time on the schema. However, prediction does not work all the time; i.e. it is not always possible to detect the changes that are plausible to occur on a database schema and are important for the database users because of the complex perception of the real world. Therefore, the predictive approach operates according to three main scenarios which are respectively:

1- Scenario 1: **Avoid redesign because better designed schema ready for evolution**
The first scenario involves the case in which the predicted schema of the database does not need to be evolved or in other words, the schema has already evolved because the required changes are already built-in and the database designer or the database administrator does not have to adjust the schema for them at the evolution time.

2- Scenario 2: **Redesign slightly because already planned so easier**
The second scenario involves the case in which the predicted schema needs to evolve. However this evolution is straightforward to realize because the required changes have already been planned and therefore need just to be added in the database schema. Consequently, in the evolution time, the schema is redesigned slightly.

3- Scenario 3: **Redesign from scratch**
The third scenario concerns the case in which the anticipated changes are not accurate for the evolution of the database scheme because somehow the potential detected future changes are not appropriate and sufficient. Consequently, in the evolution time, the database schema needs absolutely to be redesigned from scratch in order to include all the adequate changes that have occurred on it over time. This scenario raises the problem that prediction is not feasible each time and it therefore implies 1) Maybe more work since the requirements ontology needs to be updated because it does not contain the needed information. 2) However, Updating the requirements ontology may help for other future schemas redesign and evolution. For example, a case in which the government legislation means radical changes in the way tax is paid on investment interest involves changes to the investment file.

Another problem of this approach is that the effectiveness of this approach for evolution is limited by the amount and the quality of the knowledge accumulated inside the requirements ontology. Therefore, we have taken into consideration the problem of the evolution of the requirements ontology as well. For this purpose, we have adopted the multi-representation strategy based on stamping mechanism. In [13] a multi-representation solution for ontologies is presented. This solution develops a language based on description logic (DL) [14] to implement the stamping mechanism. Unfortunately, this new approach is not without problems.

Future work will proceed in both theoretical and practical directions. The theory will focus on extending the idea behind the requirements ontology and the stamping mechanism. The practical work consists in testing this approach significantly through several case studies with the use of a prototype that is under development.

References

1. Connor, R.C.H., Cutts, Q.I.: Using Persistence Technology to Control Schema Evolution. In: Proceedings of the ACM symposium on Applied computing Phoenix, Arizona. ACM Press, New York (1994)
2. Roddick, J.F: A survey of schema versioning issues for database systems. Information and Software Technology 37(7), 383–393 (1995)

3. Borgida, A., Williamson, K.E.: Accommodating Exceptions in Databases, and Refining the Schema by Learning from them. In: 11th International Conference on Very Large Data Bases, Stockholm, Sweden. Morgan Kaufmann, San Francisco (1985)
4. Benatallah, B.A: Unified Framework for Supporting Dynamic Schema Evolution in Object Database. In: Akoka, J., Bouzeghoub, M., Comyn-Wattiau, I., Métais, E. (eds.) ER 1999. LNCS, vol. 1728, Springer, Heidelberg (1999)
5. Tan, P.-N., et al.: Introduction to Data mining Pearson. Addison Wesley, Pearson (2006)
6. Sugumaran, V., Storey, V.C.: Ontologies for conceptual modeling: their creation, use, and management. Data Knowledge. Engineering 42(3), 251–271 (2002)
7. Sugumaran, V., Storey, V.C.: An Ontology-Based Framework for Generating and Improving Database Design. In: Andersson, B., Bergholtz, M., Johannesson, P. (eds.) NLDB 2002. LNCS, vol. 2553, pp. 1–12. Springer, Heidelberg (2002)
8. Kroenke, D.M.: Database Processing: Fundamentals, Design and Implementation. In: Acevedo, G.S.d. (ed.), pp. 265–275. Prentice Hall, Pearson (2004)
9. WordNet: http://wordnet.princeton.edu/
10. Lacy, L. W.: OWL: Representing Information Using the Web Ontology Language (2005)
11. Bounif, H., Pottinger, R.: Schema Repository for Database Schema Evolution. In: 2nd international workshop on Data Management in Global Data Repositories (GREP) 2006 at International Conference on Database and Expert Systems Applications 06 (2006)
12. Spaccapietra, S., et al.: Supporting Multiple Representations in Spatio-Temporal databases. In: Proceedings of the 6th EC-GI & GIS Workshop, Lyon, France, June 28-30 (2000)
13. Benslimane, D., et al.: Multi-representation in ontologies. In: Kalinichenko, L.A., Manthey, R., Thalheim, B., Wloka, U. (eds.) ADBIS 2003. LNCS, vol. 2798, pp. 4–15. Springer, Heidelberg (2003)
14. Baader, F., Nutt, W.: Basic Description Logics. In: Baader, F. (ed.) The Description Logic Handbook: theory, implementation and application, pp. 43–95. Cambridge University Press, Cambridge (2003)

Improving the Development of Data Warehouses by Enriching Dimension Hierarchies with WordNet

Jose-Norberto Mazón[1], Juan Trujillo[1], Manuel Serrano[2], and Mario Piattini[2]

[1] Dept. of Software and Computing Systems
Apto. Correos 99. E-03080
University of Alicante, Spain
{jnmazon,jtrujillo}@dlsi.ua.es
[2] Alarcos Research Group
University of Castilla-La Mancha
Paseo Universidad, 4; 13071 Ciudad Real, Spain
{Manuel.Serrano,Mario.Piattini}@uclm.es

Abstract. OLAP (On-Line Analytical Processing) operations, such as roll-up or drill-down, depend on data warehouse dimension hierarchies in order to aggregate information at different levels of detail and support the decision-making process required by final users. This is why it is crucial to capture adequate hierarchies in the requirement analysis stage. However, operational data could not be enough for supplying information to construct every level of these hierarchies. In this paper, we apply knowledge given by relationships among concepts from WordNet to overcome this problem. Therefore, richer dimension hierarchies will be specified in the data warehouse, and OLAP tools will be able to show proper information to improve decision-making process. Decision makers thus will be able to achieve their information needs for analysis. Finally, we will show the benefits of our approach by providing a case study in which a poor hierarchy is enriched with new levels of aggregation.

Keywords: Data warehouse, dimension hierarchies, WordNet.

1 Introduction

According to Inmon's definition [8], a data warehouse (DW) is "a subject oriented, integrated, non-volatile, and time variant collection of data in support of management's decision". It is widely accepted that DWs are based on multidimensional (MD) modeling which structures information into facts and dimensions. A fact contains useful measures of a business process (sales, deliveries, etc.), whereas a dimension represents the context for analyzing a fact (product, customer, time, etc.) by means of hierarchically organized dimension attributes [26]. These dimension hierarchies are of paramount importance in OLAP (On-Line Analytical Processing) tools. These tools are commonly used to support the decision-making process, by allowing users to analyze the large amount of data stored in the DW. In this analysis, operations such as roll-up or drill-down are used to aggregate or disaggregate data, depending on levels of aggregation which must be explicitly

M. Collard (Ed.): ODBIS 2005/2006, LNCS 4623, pp. 85–101, 2007.

specified by organizing the members of a given dimension into hierarchies [2,9,12,15,21,22,26]. Thus, hierarchies must be properly defined for analyzing data stored in DW according to user requirements in order to improve the decision-making process. In fact, the richer a hierarchy is defined, the more meaningful users' queries will be answered and the better decisions will be made.

Lately, we have been defining an approach [12,30], based on the UML (Unified Modeling Language) [20] and the i* notation [31] for the development of DWs from user requirements and data sources. Within this approach, once user requirements are correctly captured, we obtain the corresponding MD conceptual schema (i.e. required MD schema). The required MD schema is then conformed to the operational sources that will populate the DW by using a set of multidimensional normal forms in order to assure certain desirable properties, such as faithfulness, completeness or avoidance of redundancies [32]. Nevertheless, in this conformation process, we found that the required MD schema could not be totally specified as many MD elements do not have their counterpart on the operational data sources and only a reduced version of this schema was obtained: the conformed MD schema [41]. One of the major constraints in this conformed MD schema is the fact that the levels of aggregation of the dimension hierarchies are restricted by the available data sources, and then the required levels of aggregation could not be specified in the schema.

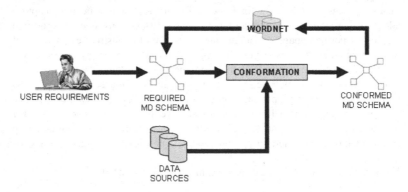

Fig. 1. Using WordNet to enrich the conformed MD schema

Consequently, data sources may not be enough to obtain required hierarchies and DW users can only analyze data by using conformed hierarchies[1]. Therefore, the final DW will not completely satisfy final user requirements. Thus, in this paper we present an approach to enrich conformed dimension hierarchies by adding new levels of aggregation in order to obtain the required hierarchies, even although available data sources are not enough to provide the required MD elements. DW users will thus satisfy their analysis needs. To accomplish this, we propose the use of semantic relations among concepts provided by WordNet [16]. The initial hypothesis is that both DWs and WordNet present hierarchical structures: dimension hierarchies in

---

[1] We regard required hierarchies to be those obtained from end user requirements (i.e. they are part of the required MD schema); while conformed hierarchies are those that conform to the data provided by operational sources (i.e. they are part of the conformed MD schema).

DWs show the relationships between value domains from different dimension attributes [1,2,12,15,21,22,23] (set by levels of aggregation), while WordNet presents hierarchical semantic relations between concepts, such as hypernymy/hyponymy or meronymy/holonymy [16,17]. Therefore, our approach is based on using these WordNet relations to add new levels to conformed dimension hierarchies in order to obtain the required hierarchies. Figure 1 summarizes this scenario.

The benefit of our proposal is clear: using knowledge provided by WordNet to ameliorate the development of DWs, since the quality of dimension hierarchies is improved by means of adding new hierarchy aggregation levels, which allow DW users to achieve their analysis information needs and, in this way, to better support the decision-making process.

The remainder of this paper is structured as follows. Section 2 presents an overview of works about the development of DWs and the use of WordNet and ontologies in the development of information systems. Section 3 describes our approach for modeling DWs and their dimension hierarchies based on UML. Section 4 overviews WordNet. Section 5 defines our approach for enriching dimension hierarchies using WordNet. In section 6, a case study is presented. Finally, we point out our conclusions and sketch some future work in Section 7.

2 Related Work

It is widely accepted that the development of DWs must be based on the conceptual modeling of the main MD properties. Therefore, in this section, we focus on briefly describing the most relevant approaches for the conceptual modeling of DWs and, more generally, the use of ontologies and WordNet in conceptual modeling.

2.1 Conceptual Modeling of DWs

Various approaches for the conceptual design of DW systems have been proposed in the last few years. In this section, we present a brief discussion about some of the most well-known approaches.

In [11], different case studies of data marts (DM) are presented. The DW design is based on the use of the star schema and its different variations (snowflake and fact constellation). Moreover, the BUS matrix architecture is proposed to build a corporate DW by integrating the design of several DMs. Although we consider this work as a fundamental reference in the MD field, we miss a formal approach for dealing, in an integrated way, with both user requirements and data sources in the development of DWs.

In [37], authors propose the Dimensional-Fact Model (DFM), a particular notation for the DW conceptual design. Moreover, they also propose how to derive a DW schema from the data sources described by Entity-Relationship (ER) schemas. From our point of view, this proposal assumes that ER schemas contain all the required information for build a DW which provides data in a suitable way for achieving user analysis needs. Unfortunately, some important terms and data could be missing from the data sources and some external sources could be needed.

In [38], authors present the Multidimensional Model, a logical model for OLAP systems, and show how it can be used in the design of MD databases. Authors also propose a general design method, aimed at building a MD schema starting from an operational database described by an ER schema. Although the design steps are described in a logic and coherent way, the DW design is only based on the operational data sources, what we consider insufficient because some user analysis needs could not be accomplished unless other data sources are used.

In [39], the building of star schemas (and its different variations) from the conceptual schemas of the operational data sources is proposed. Once again, it is highly supposed that the required information for constructing the DW comes only from the available data sources.

Every of the above-described approaches present the following main drawback: they consider the available data sources enough for specifying a DW which provides proper information to allows decision makers to achieve their analysis needs. However, decision makers could improve their analysis needs if other sources are considered. This must be taken into account in early stages of the development process, i.e. conceptual modeling of the DWs.

2.2 Ontologies and WordNet in Conceptual Modeling

Traditionally, WordNet has been used to improve natural language processing systems. It has supported several kinds of tasks, such as information retrieval and extraction, document structuring and categorization, etc. A comprehensive review of applications related to WordNet can be found in [19].

On the other hand, ontologies have been successfully used for conceptual modeling. In [33], authors apply named entity recognition and ontologies to database prototyping process and sample data.

In [34], authors present a framework for supporting the generation and analysis of conceptual database designs through the use of ontologies. This paper demonstrates how the use of domain knowledge stored in the form of an ontology can be useful to assist in the generation of more complete and consistent database designs, both for design generation and design verification.

In [35], authors present experiments designed to assess the extent to which a natural language processing tool improves the quality of conceptual models, specifically object-oriented ones.

The work presented in [36] proposes a UML profile for ontology representation and conceptual modeling. Authors point out that a conceptual modeling language should be founded on formal upper-level ontologies to be able to model reality. They show the relevance of the tools proposed by applying them to solve recurrent problems in the practice of conceptual modeling.

Within multidimensional environments, ontologies have been specially used for data integration. The work presented in [10] uses linguistic knowledge provided by ontologies during the process of data cleaning in multisource information systems to solve terminological conflicts between data instances. In this work, authors advocate the use of WordNet. In [27], authors present an ontology-based method to find suitable data from different sources and to semantically integrate them into one OLAP cube. A review of the use of ontologies for data integration can be found in [29]. For a more general review, we refer reader to [3].

Finally, we would like to point out that although several works [2,9,15] have paid attention to the importance of dimension hierarchies in DWs, to the best of our knowledge, our contribution is the first work about employing ontologies for improving the design of dimension hierarchies in DWs.

3 Using UML for Data Warehouse Modeling

Multidimensional databases, OLAP applications, and DWs provide companies with many years of historical information for the decision-making process. It is widely accepted that these systems are based on multidimensional (MD) modeling which structures information into facts and dimensions. A fact contains interesting measures (fact attributes) of a business process (sales, deliveries, etc.), whereas a dimension represents the context for analyzing a fact (product, customer, time, etc.) by means of dimension attributes hierarchically organized. A set of fact measures is based on a set of dimensions that determine the granularity adopted for representing facts.

In this paper, we follow our object oriented approach for the development of conceptual models of DWs [12]. This approach has been specified by means of a UML profile that contains the necessary stereotypes in order to successfully represent the MD properties in a UML class diagram [20]. In this diagram, the information is clearly organized into facts and dimensions represented by means of fact classes and dimension classes respectively (see Table 1).

Fact classes are defined as composite classes in shared aggregation relationships of n dimension classes. The minimum cardinality in the role of the dimension classes is 1 to indicate that all the facts must always be related to all the dimensions. The relations "many-to-many" between a fact and a specific dimension are specified by means of the cardinality 1...* in the role of the corresponding dimension class. A fact is composed of measures or fact attributes. By default, all measures in the fact class are considered to be additive. For non-additive measures, additive rules are defined as constraints and are included in the fact class. Furthermore, derived measures can also be explicitly represented (indicated by /) and their derivation rules are placed between braces near the fact class.

Regarding dimensions, there are two kinds of hierarchies: classification hierarchies, represented by association relationships, and categorization hierarchies, represented by means of generalization relationships.

Classification hierarchies defined on certain dimension attributes are crucial because the subsequent data analysis will be addressed by these hierarchies. A dimension attribute may also be aggregated (related) to more than one hierarchy, and therefore multiple classification hierarchies and alternative path hierarchies are also relevant. For this reason, a common way of representing and considering dimensions with their classification hierarchies is using Directed Acyclic Graphs (DAG). Nevertheless, classification hierarchies are not so simple in most of the cases. The concepts of "strictness" and "completeness" are important, not only for conceptual purposes, but also for further steps of MD modeling. "Strictness" means that an object of a lower level of hierarchy belongs to only one of higher level, e.g. a *city* is only related to one *state*. "Completeness" means that all members belong to one higher class object and that object consists only of those members. For example, suppose we say that the classification hierarchy between the *state* and the *city* levels is "complete". In this case, a *state* is formed by all *cities* recorded and all the *cities* that form the *state* are recorded. In our MD conceptual model, each level of a classification hierarchy is specified by a base class (see Table 1). An association of base classes specifies the relationship between two levels of a classification hierarchy. The only prerequisite is that these classes must define a DAG rooted in the dimension class.

Lastly, categorization hierarchies are useful when OLAP scenarios become very large as the number of dimensions increases significantly. This fact may lead to extremely sparse dimensions and data cubes. In this way, there are attributes that are normally valid for all elements within a dimension while others are only valid for a subset of elements. For example, attributes *number of passengers* and *number of airbags* would only be valid for *cars* and will be *"null"* for *vans*. In our MD conceptual model, categorization hierarchies are considered by means of the generalization/specialization relationships of UML.

Table 1. Class stereotypes of our UML profile to be used in this paper

Stereotype	Description	Icon
Fact class	Represent facts consisting of measures	
Dimension class	Represent dimensions consisting of hierarchy levels	
Base class	Represent dimension hierarchy levels and their attributes	/B/

Once the structure of the MD model has been defined, final users require fulfilling a set of initial analysis requirements as a starting point for the subsequent analysis phase. From these initial requirements, users can apply a set of operations (OLAP operations) to the MD view of data for further analysis. OLAP operations related to dimension hierarchies are usually as following: roll-up (increasing the level of aggregation) and drill-down (decreasing the level of aggregation) along one or more classification hierarchies.

4 WordNet

WordNet [16] is a linguistic resource that provides lexical information about words and their senses. Furthermore, WordNet also provides a variety of semantic relations which are defined between concepts [17], so it can be used like an ontology. Syntactic category of each word determines its potential semantic relationships. In this paper, we focus on noun semantic relations (since dimension attributes are usually nouns) namely:

- Synonymy: it is a symmetric relation between word forms. It is a similar relationship: synonymy indicates that two concepts have a similar meaning. For example: *pipe* and *tube* are synonyms.
- Antonymy: it is also a symmetric relation between word forms. It is an opposite relationship: antonymy indicates that two concepts have an opposite meaning. For example: *hell* and *heaven* are antonyms.
- Hyponymy/Hypernymy: they represent transitive relations between concepts. It is a subtype/supertype relationship. Giving two concepts X and Y, it is expressed as X is-a-kind-of Y, where X is a more specific concept (hyponym) and Y is a more generic concept (hypernym). An example: *cake* is-a-kind-of *baked goods*. In Fig. 2, an example of a more comprehensive hypernym hierarchy is given: *chocolate cake* is-a-kind-of *cake*, which is-a-kind-of *baked goods*, which is-a-kind-of *food*.
- Meronymy/Holonymy: they are complex semantic relations, such as components parts, substantive parts, and member parts. They are whole-part relationships. Giving two concepts X and Y, it is expressed as X is-a-part-of Y, where X is a concept that represents a part (meronym) of whole concept Y (holonym). For example: *wheel* is-a-part-of *car*.

```
chocolate cake -- (cake containing chocolate)
    => cake -- (made from or based on a mixture of flour and sugar
    and eggs)
        => baked goods -- (foods (like breads and cakes and
        pastries) that are cooked in an oven)
            => food -- (any solid substance (as opposed to liquid) that
            is used as a source of nourishment; "food and drink")
```

Fig. 2. Hypernym hierarchy for *chocolate cake*

These semantic relations allow us to organize concepts into hierarchical structures (an example of a hypernym hierarchy is shown in Fig. 2). In particular we are interested in hypernymy ("is-a-kind-of" or generalization) and meronymy ("is-a-part-of" or aggregation) relations between nouns; since, they are the most useful relationships in a dimension hierarchy [1,2,12,15,22].

To sum up, in our approach, WordNet is used because it provides concepts from many domains, and it presents relations between these concepts which are easy to understand and use. Furthermore, it can be easily extended to other languages, apart from English, by means of EuroWordNet [28].

5 Using WordNet to Enrich Dimension Hierarchies

Dimension hierarchies in DWs show the relationships between domains of values from different dimension attributes (set in levels of aggregation). As above-described, WordNet also presents hierarchy relationships between concepts, such as hypernymy/hyponymy and meronymy/holonymy. Thereby, we will use this hierarchical organization of WordNet to automatically complete dimension hierarchies.

We focus on the dimension hierarchy definition provided by [12], described in section 3. Since UML is used for designing a DW, hierarchies are modeled by using UML relationships. Particularly for classification hierarchies we use associations (including aggregations) between levels and generalizations for categorization hierarchies. For generalization we will use hypernymy/hyponymy relationship provided by WordNet. Association relationship from UML is more general, since it only specifies that two elements are connected. Thus, we will use hypernymy/hyponymy or meronymy/holonymy relationships from WordNet depending on the domain of dimension attributes: if an association is considered as an aggregation then we use meronymy/holonymy, else we use hypernymy/hyponymy. For example, in the case of the hierarchy *city-state-country,* we will use meronymy/holonymy relationship due to the fact that *city* is a part of *state* and *state* is a part of *country* (e.g. *Boston* is a part of *Massachusetts* and *Massachusetts* is a part of *USA*). However, if the hierarchy is *product-family-class*, hypernymy/hyponymy relationships will be used, because of every *product* is a kind of *family* and every *family* is a kind of *class* (e.g. *cake* is a kind of *baked good* and *baked good* is a kind of *food*).

For the sake of clarity when explaining our proposal, from now on, we assume that only strict hierarchies are taken into account. So, non-strict hierarchies are not considered. It can be assumed because of WordNet restrictions regarding relationships, since there is usually only one hypernym for each word sense [4,16].

Our approach consists of grouping word senses whose hypernyms/meronyms are equal, into a new set of word senses. This new set corresponds to a level of a dimension hierarchy. Each set of senses is described by its common hypernym/meronym. In order to create another level in a hierarchy, grouping again into hypernym/meronym senses (by its common upper concept) is required until the needed level of aggregation is achieved. Before starting, word senses must be disambiguated to obtain the right sense for each one. For disambiguation we have based on specification marks WSD (Word Sense Disambiguation) algorithm from [18], since it offers good results when every word for disambiguating belongs to the same domain[2].

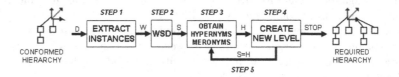

Fig. 3. Overview of our approach

Following, we explain the main steps of our approach (an overview is shown in Fig. 3):

Prerequisite 1. A dimension attribute (denoted as *D*) is chosen from a conformed hierarchy. The dimension hierarchy will be enriched starting from this attribute.

---

[2] We assume that every possible value of a certain dimension attribute belongs to the same domain. For example, all possible values of the attribute *city* will be *names of cities*.

Prerequisite 2. A level of aggregation (called a) is specified. This is the number of aggregation levels required to properly analyze data from the DW.

Prerequisite 3. Create a variable t. This variable increments its value when a new level of aggregation is created. It must be initialized: $t=0$.

Step 1. Extract all values (without repeating any value) from chosen dimension attribute. These values are nouns and they constitute the input (or context) for specification marks WSD algorithm:

$$W=\{w_1, w_2, ..., w_n\};\ where\ w_i\ denotes\ every\ value\ of\ the\ selected\ dimension\ attribute$$

Step 2. For each word in W, we have to obtain its correct senses from WordNet using specification mark WSD. Here s_i represents the correct sense for context value w_i.

$$S=\{s_1, s_2, ..., s_n\};\ where\ s_i\ is\ the\ sense\ of\ w_i$$

Step 3. For each sense in S, we obtain one hypernym/meronym (only the lowest one) as h_i.

$$H_{si}=\{h_i\}\ \forall s_i \in S,\ h_i\ is\ the\ lowest\ hypernym/meronym\ of\ s_i$$

The set of every hypernym/meronym senses obtaining from every H_{si} without repeating is also formed:

$$H=\{h_1, h_2, ..., h_n\}$$

Step 4. A new hierarchy level is created and every hypernym/meronym sense from H_{si} is added as instance.

Step 5. Take new input values as all hypernym/meronym senses: $S=H$.

Stop condition. $t=t+1$. If the required level of aggregation is reached ($t=a$) or S has only one element (all input attributes already have a common hypernym/ meronym), then the maximum level of aggregation has been reached for these input values. Otherwise, go to step 3.

In Fig. 3, every step of our approach is illustrated. From a conformed dimension hierarchy in a MD model which not accomplishes user requirements because it does not have enough levels of aggregation, a dimension attribute is chosen and all its values form the context for specification marks WSD algorithm in order to obtain right senses for each value of dimension attributes. Afterwards, iterations start to obtain hypernyms/meronyms of values, a new level of the dimension hierarchy is created, and values are mapped into this new level of the hierarchy. Iterations are repeated until the required dimension hierarchy, with every needed level of aggregation, is obtained.

6 Case Study

In this section, we will show the benefits of our approach by providing a little case study in which a conformed hierarchy is enriched with new levels of aggregation. Our case study consists of a retail sales business composed of several grocery stores spread over several regions. In each store several products are sold. This business process deals with analyzing which products have been sold in which stores on what date. The store manager needs to further study these sales, analyzing them by means of several levels of aggregation (e.g. user needs to analyze the sales aggregating by classes of product), which must be specified in the required dimension hierarchy (see Fig. 4). However, only name of the product is available in the operational sources (see Table 2), so after the conformation process, the conformed hierarchy only consists of one level: *product* (see Fig. 5).

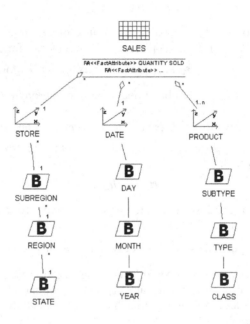

Fig. 4. Required MD schema (according to user requirements)

Conformed dimension hierarchies are shown in Fig. 5. We can see that product dimension has not enough levels to accomplish user requirements. Since user requirements are not achieved by this conformed hierarchy, we apply the approach above-described to introduce new levels in the dimension hierarchy and enrich it. Conformed hierarchy consists of an aggregation level, named *product* (see Fig. 5). However, decision makers need to aggregate data in three more levels (according to the required hierarchy in Fig. 4): a lower level called *subtype*, an intermediate level called *type* and a higher level called *class* (see figure 4). Three new levels have to be added to the conformed hierarchy in order to enrich it, thus obtaining the required one. We consider that the user knows the semantic of each level, so levels will be denoted as *level 1*, *level 2*, and *level 3*.

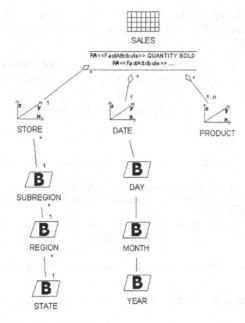

Fig. 5. Conformed MD schema

Now, every step to obtain the required hierarchy from the conformed one is described:

Prerequisite 1. Dimension attribute *product* is chosen (see Table 2).

Prerequisite 2. Three new levels of aggregation are required, so $a=3$.

Prerequisite 3. $t=0$.

Table 2. Some of data stored in the operational data sources

Quantity	Product	Date
2	*Bourbon*	17/01/2002
3	*Merlot*	01/02/2002
2	*Chardonnay*	03/02/2002
2	*Cabernet*	10/01/2002
1	*Scotch*	09/02/2002

Step 1. Input values are the following:

$$W=\{bourbon, merlot, chardonnay, cabernet, scotch\}$$

Step 2. For each word in the input, its correct senses using specification marks WSD are the following:

$$S=\{s_1, s_2, s_3, s_4, s_5\}=\{bourbon\#2, merlot\#2, chardonnay\#2, cabernet\#1, scotch\#1\}$$

Step 3. Hypernyms for each sense of S are obtained from WordNet (only the lowest hypernym for each sense). Fig. 6 shows an example of hypernym path of the concept *bourbon* with sense *#2*.

$$H_{bourbon\#2}=\{whisky\#1\},\ H_{merlot\#2}=\{red\ wine\#1\},$$
$$H_{chardonnay\#2}=\{white\ wine\#1\},\ H_{cabernet\#1}=\{red\ wine\#1\},$$
$$H_{scotch\#2}=\{whisky\#1\}$$
$$H=\{whisky\#1,\ red\ wine\#1,\ white\ wine\#1\}$$

Sense 2
bourbon -- (whiskey distilled from a mash of corn and malt and rye and aged in charred oak barrels)
    => whiskey, whisky -- (a liquor made from fermented mash of grain)
      => liquor, spirits, booze, hard drink, hard liquor, John Barleycorn, strong drink -- (distilled rather than fermented)
        => alcohol, alcoholic beverage, intoxicant, inebriant -- (a liquor or brew containing alcohol as the active agent; "alcohol (or drink) ruined him")

Fig. 6. Hypernym path of the concept *bourbon* from our case study

Step 4. Level 1 is added (see Table 3).

Table 3. First created hierarchy level and its mapped values

Product	Level 1
Bourbon	*Whisky*
Merlot	*Red wine*
Chardonnay	*White wine*
Cabernet	*Red wine*
Scotch	*Whisky*

Step 5. Definition of new values for S:

$$S=H=\{whisky\#1,\ red\ wine\#1,\ white\ wine\#1\}$$

Stop condition. $t=1$. $t<a$, then go to *step 3*.

Step 3. Hypernyms for each sense of S are obtained:

$$H_{whisky\#1}=\{liquor\#1\},\ H_{red\ wine\#1}=\{wine\#1\},$$
$$H_{white\ wine\#1}=\{wine\#1\}$$
$$H=\{liquor\#1,\ wine\#1\}$$

Step 4. Level 2 is added (see Table 4).

Step 5. S=H={liquor#1, wine#1}.

Stop condition. $t=2$. $t<a$ then go to *step 3*.

Step 3. Hypernyms for each sense of *S* are obtained

$$H_{liquor\#1}=\{alcohol\#1\}, H_{wine\#1}=\{alcohol\#1\}$$
$$H=\{alcohol\#1\}$$

Step 4. Level 3 is added (see Table 5).

Step 5. S=H={alcohol#1}.

Stop condition. *t=3=a* then *stop*.

Table 4. First and second levels created and its values

Product	Level 1	Level 2
Bourbon	*Whisky*	*Liquor*
Merlot	*Red wine*	*Wine*
Chardonnay	*White wine*	*Wine*
Cabernet	*Red wine*	*Wine*
Scotch	*Whisky*	*Liquor*

Table 5. Hierarchy levels created by our approach and its values

Product	Level 1	Level 2	Level 3
Bourbon	*Whisky*	*Liquor*	*Alcohol*
Merlot	*Red wine*	*Wine*	*Alcohol*
Chardonnay	*White wine*	*Wine*	*Alcohol*
Cabernet	*Red wine*	*Wine*	*Alcohol*
Scotch	*Whisky*	*Liquor*	*Alcohol*

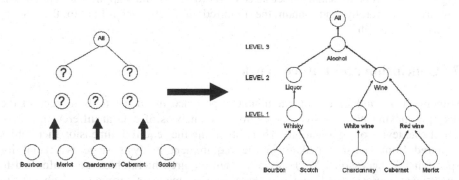

Fig. 7. Instances before and after applying our approach

After applying our approach, an enriched hierarchy is obtained (see Fig. 4 and Table 5) which accomplishes user requirements: *analyzing quantity of product sold aggregating by several hierarchy levels (subtype, type, and class of product)*, despite only one level of aggregation (*product*) was available in the operational data sources. Then, our approach was applied starting with a conformed hierarchy (see Fig. 5 and

Table 2) only with one level of aggregation (*product*) and the required hierarchy has been obtained by adding the following aggregation levels: *subtype*, *type*, and *class* of product). This enriched hierarchy is shown in Fig. 4, while its instances can be both observed in Table 5 and Fig. 7.

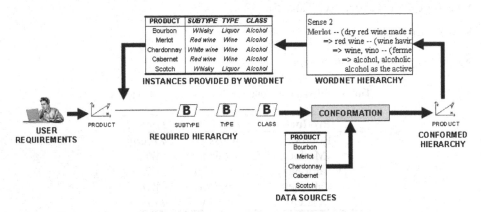

Fig. 8. An example of using WordNet in our overall proposal for the development of DWs

Fig. 8 shows an example (based on our case study) about how WordNet is applied within our overall proposal for the development of DWs: a user requirement states that a quantity of sold product must be analyzed according to several aggregation levels (*subtype*, *type*, and *class* of product). Therefore, a hierarchy is specified according to this requirement (i.e. required hierarchy). However, only the name of the product is available from the data sources. Thus, when the required hierarchy is conformed to these sources, the resulting conformed hierarchy does not have enough aggregation levels to satisfy user needs. WordNet is then applied to enrich this conformed hierarchy and obtain the required hierarchy according to the above-described approach.

7 Conclusion and Future Work

Dimension hierarchies are of paramount importance in OLAP tools to support the decision making process, since they allow the analysis of data at different levels of detail (i.e. levels of aggregation). Then, obtaining the required dimension hierarchies captured from decision makers in the requirement analysis stage is crucial for specifying a successful DW. However, when required hierarchies are conformed to operational sources, we found that these sources may not provide enough data to construct every level of required hierarchies, meaning that only conformed hierarchies can be obtained. Therefore, user requirements are not satisfied, as conformed hierarchies may not deliver the expected information to support the decision-making process. In this paper, we have proposed the application of WordNet to obtain the required hierarchies. The advantage of our proposal is clear: the enrichment of conformed hierarchies by adding new aggregation levels in order to satisfy the required hierarchies. These required hierarchies allow DW users to satisfy their information analysis needs, since they better support the decision-making process.

In spite of using WordNet, we have to point out that it presents several ontological problems [4] which must be overcome in a next future. For instance, WordNet does not have enough relations, such as attribution ("is-an-attribute-of") [24], which could be used to enrich every level of the hierarchy by adding several possible attributes (i.e. for *city*, attributes like *population* or *area* could be added). Some kind of formal specification of WordNet (like OntoWordNet [5]) could be used to solve these ontological problems.

Just as the work presented in [25], we can study a methodology for creating and managing domain ontologies to properly apply them in our approach.

Finally, we can use WordNet within DWs systems to overcome dimension update problems [7] or to resolve integration problems [10] and inaccuracy problems regarding summarizability [6,40].

Acknowledgments. This work has been partially supported by the METASIGN (TIN2004-00779) project from the Spanish Ministry of Education and Science, by the DADASMECA project (GV05/220) from the Valencia Ministry of Enterprise, University and Science (Spain), and by the DADS (PBC-05-012-2) project from the Castilla-La Mancha Ministry of Education and Science (Spain). Jose-Norberto Mazón is funded by the Spanish Ministry of Education and Science under a FPU grant (AP2005-1360).

References

1. Abelló, A., Samos, J., Saltor, F.: Understanding Analysis Dimensions in a Multidimensional Object-Oriented Model. In: Int. Workshop on Design and Management of Data Warehouses (DMDW) (2001)
2. Akoka, J., Comyn-Wattiau, I., Prat, N.: Dimension Hierarchies Design from UML Generalizations and Aggregations. In: Kunii, H.S., Jajodia, S., Sølvberg, A. (eds.) ER 2001. LNCS, vol. 2224, pp. 442–455. Springer, Heidelberg (2001)
3. Chandrasekaran, B., Josephson, J.R., Benjamins, V.R.: Ontologies: What are they? why do we need them? IEEE Intelligent Systems and Their Applications 14(1), 20–26 (1999)
4. Gangemi, A., Guarino, N., Masolo, C., Oltramari, A.: Sweetening WORDNET with DOLCE. AI Magazine 24(3), 13–24 (2003)
5. Gangemi, A., Navigli, R., Velardi, P.: The OntoWordNet Project: Extension and Axiomatization of Conceptual Relations in WordNet. In: Meersman, R., Tari, Z., Schmidt, D.C. (eds.) CoopIS 2003, DOA 2003, and ODBASE 2003. LNCS, vol. 2888, pp. 820–838. Springer, Heidelberg (2003)
6. Horner, J., Song, I.-Y., Chen, P.: An analysis of additivity in OLAP systems. In: 7th ACM Int. Workshop on Data Warehousing and OLAP (DOLAP), pp. 83–91. ACM Press, New York (2004)
7. Hurtado, C.A., Mendelzon, A.O., Vaisman, A.A.: Maintaining Data Cubes under Dimension Updates. In: 15th International Conference on Data Engineering (ICDE), pp. 346–355. IEEE Computer Society Press, Los Alamitos (1999)
8. Inmon, W.: Building the Data warehouse. John Wiley & Sons, Chichester (1996)

9. Jagadish, H.V., Lakshmanan, L.V.S., Srivastava, D.: What can Hierarchies do for Data Warehouses? In: 25th VLDB Conference (1999)
10. Kedad, Z., Métais, E.: Ontology-Based Data Cleaning. In: Andersson, B., Bergholtz, M., Johannesson, P. (eds.) NLDB 2002. LNCS, vol. 2553, pp. 137–149. Springer, Heidelberg (2002)
11. Kimball, R.: The Data Warehouse Toolkit: Practical Techniques For Building Dimensional Data Warehouse. John Wiley & Sons, Chichester (1996)
12. Luján-Mora, S., Trujillo, J., Song, I.-Y.: A UML Profile for Multidimensional Modeling in Data Warehouses. Data & Knowledge Engineering 59(3), 725–769 (2006)
13. Luján-Mora, S., Trujillo, J.: A Comprehensive Method for Data Warehouse Design. In: Proceedings of the 5th International Workshop on Design and Management of Data Warehouses (DMDW'03), Berlin, Germany, pp. 1.1–1.14 (September 2003)
14. Luján-Mora, S., Trujillo, J.: A Data Warehouse Engineering Process. In: Yakhno, T. (ed.) ADVIS 2004. LNCS, vol. 3261, pp. 14–23. Springer, Heidelberg (2004)
15. Malinowski, E., Zimányi, E.: OLAP Hierarchies: A Conceptual Perspective. In: Persson, A., Stirna, J. (eds.) CAiSE 2004. LNCS, vol. 3084, pp. 477–491. Springer, Heidelberg (2004)
16. Miller, G.A., Beckwith, R., Fellbaum, C., Gross, D., Miller, K.J.: WordNet: An on-line lexical database. International Journal of Lexicography 3(4) (1990)
17. Miller, G.A., Fellbaum, C.: Semantic networks of English. Lexical And Conceptual Semantics. Blackwell Cambridge and Oxford. England, pp. 197–229 (1992)
18. Montoyo, A., Palomar, M.: WSD Algorithm Applied to a NLP System. In: Bouzeghoub, M., Kedad, Z., Métais, E. (eds.) NLDB 2000. LNCS, vol. 1959, pp. 54–65. Springer, Heidelberg (2001)
19. Morato, J., Marzal, M.A., Lloréns, J., Moreiro, J.: WordNet Applications. In: Proc. of the 2nd International WordNet Conference (GWC), pp. 270–278 (2004)
20. Object Management Group (OMG). Unified Modeling Language Specification 1.5 (2004), http://www.omg.org/cgi-bin/doc?formal/03-03-01
21. Pourabbas, E., Rafanelli, M.: Characterization of Hierarchies and Some Operators in OLAP Environment. In: Proc. of the 2nd ACM Int. Workshop on Data Warehousing and OLAP (DOLAP), pp. 54–59. ACM Press, New York (1999)
22. Schneider, M.: Well-formed Data Warehouses Structures. In: 5th International Workshop Design and Management of Data Warehouses (2003)
23. Smith, J.M., Smith, D.C.P.: Database Abstractions: Aggregations and Generalizations. ACM TODS 2(2) (1977)
24. Storey, V.: Understanding Semantic Relationships. VLDB Journal 2, 455–488 (1993)
25. Sugumaran, V., Storey, V.: Ontologies for conceptual modeling: their creation, use, and management. Data & Knowledge Engineering 42(3), 251–271 (2002)
26. Trujillo, J., Palomar, M., Gómez, J., Song, I.Y.: Designing Data Warehouses with OO Conceptual Models. IEEE Computer 34(12), 66–75 (2001)
27. Toivonen, S., Niemi, T.: Describing data sources semantically for facilitating efficient creation of OLAP cubes. In: McIlraith, S.A., Plexousakis, D., van Harmelen, F. (eds.) ISWC 2004. LNCS, vol. 3298. Springer, Heidelberg (2004)
28. Vossen, P.: EuroWordNet: building a multilingual database with wordnets for European languages, vol. 3(1), pp. 7–10. Published in: The ELRA Newsletter, Paris (February 1998) ISSN: 1026-8300
29. Wache, H., Vögele, T., Visser, U., Stuckenschmidt, H., Schuster, G., Neumann, H., Hübner, S.: Ontology-based integration of information – A survey of existing approaches. In: Proceedings of IJCAI-01. Workshop: Ontologies and Information Sharing, Seattle, WA, pp. 108–117 (2001)

30. Mazón, J.-N., Trujillo, J., Serrano, M., Piattini, M.: Designing Data Warehouses: from Business Requirement Analysis to Multidimensional Modeling. In: Int. Workshop on Requirements Engineering for Business Needs and IT Alignment, REBNITA (2005)
31. Yu, E.: Modeling Strategic Relationships for Process Reenginering, Ph.D. Thesis. University of Toronto (1995)
32. Mazón, J.-N., Trujillo, J., Lechtenbörger, J.: A Set of QVT Relations to Assure the Correctness of Data Warehouses by Using Multidimensional Normal Forms. In: Embley, D.W., Olivé, A., Ram, S. (eds.) ER 2006. LNCS, vol. 4215, pp. 385–398. Springer, Heidelberg (2006)
33. Moreda, P., Muñoz, R., Martínez-Barco, P., Cachero, C., Palomar, M.: A web information extraction system to DB prototyping. In: Andersson, B., Bergholtz, M., Johannesson, P. (eds.) NLDB 2002. LNCS, vol. 2553, pp. 13–26. Springer, Heidelberg (2002)
34. Sugumaran, V., Storey, V.: An Ontology-Based Framework for Generating and Improving Database Design. In: Andersson, B., Bergholtz, M., Johannesson, P. (eds.) NLDB 2002. LNCS, vol. 2553, pp. 1–12. Springer, Heidelberg (2002)
35. Kiyavitskaya, N., Zeni1, N., Mich, L., Mylopoulos, J.: Experimenting with Linguistic Tools for Conceptual Modeling: Quality of the Models and Critical Features. In: Meziane, F., Métais, E. (eds.) NLDB 2004. LNCS, vol. 3136, pp. 135–146. Springer, Heidelberg (2004)
36. Guizzardi, G., Wagner, G., Guarino, N., van Sinderen, M.: An Ontologically Well-Founded Profile for UML Conceptual Models. In: Persson, A., Stirna, J. (eds.) CAiSE 2004. LNCS, vol. 3084, pp. 112–126. Springer, Heidelberg (2004)
37. Golfarelli, M., Maio, D., Rizzi, S.: The Dimensional Fact Model: A Conceptual Model for Data Warehouses. Int. J. Cooperative Inf. Syst. 7(2-3), 215–247 (1998)
38. Cabibbo, L., Torlone, R.: A Logical Approach to Multidimensional Databases. In: Schek, H.-J., Saltor, F., Ramos, I., Alonso, G. (eds.) EDBT 1998. LNCS, vol. 1377, pp. 183–197. Springer, Heidelberg (1998)
39. Tryfona, N., Busborg, F., Christiansen, J.: starER: A Conceptual Model for Data Warehouse Design. In: Proc. Of the ACM 2nd Intl. Workshop on Data Warehousing and OLAP (DOLAP'99), Kansas City, USA. ACM Press, New York (1999)
40. Horner, J., Song, I.-Y.: A Taxonomy of Inaccurate Summaries and Their Management in OLAP Systems. In: Delcambre, L.M.L., Kop, C., Mayr, H.C., Mylopoulos, J., Pastor, Ó. (eds.) ER 2005. LNCS, vol. 3716, pp. 433–448. Springer, Heidelberg (2005)
41. Mazón, J.-N., Trujillo, J.: Enriching Data Warehouse Dimension Hierarchies by Using Semantic Relations. In: Bell, D., Hong, J. (eds.) Flexible and Efficient Information Handling. LNCS, vol. 4042, pp. 278–281. Springer, Heidelberg (2006)

Management of Large Spatial Ontology Bases

Evangelos Dellis and Georgios Paliouras

Institute of Informatics & Telecommunications,
National Centre for Scientific Research "Demokritos",
15310 Ag. Paraskevi, Athens, Greece
{dellis,paliourg}@iit.demokritos.gr

Abstract. In this paper we propose a method for efficient management of large spatial ontologies. Current spatial ontologies are usually represented using an ontology language, such as OWL and stored as OWL files. However, we have observed some shortcomings using this approach especially in the efficiency of spatial query processing. This fact motivated the development of a hybrid approach that uses an R-tree as a spatial index structure. In this way we are able to support efficient query processing over large spatial ontologies, maintaining the benefits of ontological reasoning. We present a case study for emergency teams during Search and Rescue (SaR) operations showing how an Ontology Data Service (SHARE-ODS) can benefit from a spatial index. Performance evaluation shows the superiority of our proposed technique compared to the original approach. To the best of our knowledge, this is the first attempt to address the problem of efficient management of large spatial ontology bases.

Keywords: Spatial Databases, Ontologies, Knowledge Bases.

1 Introduction

The SHARE project[1] develops a Push-To-Share (PTS) advanced mobile service that provides communication support for emergency teams during Search and Rescue (SaR) operations. SaR operations are conducted by fire-brigade, rescue and medical units, operating under a complex unified command-and-communications structure. The SHARE Ontology Data Service (SHARE-ODS) [1], [2] which supports the PTS service, combines multimedia semantic modeling and spatio-temporal modeling in a unified ontology. A model for the semantic indexing of multimedia objects in the context of SaR processes and activities is also proposed in [1], [2]. This model unifies the various aspects of a SaR operation, while allowing the semantic cross-checking of possibly-unreliable information automatically extracted from multimedia objects.

Ontologies represent concepts, relations among them and instances. Commonly, an ontology consists of a relatively small conceptual part (TBox in Description Logic terminology) and a much larger instance base (ABox in Description Logic terminology), or a dense combination of concepts, relations and

---

[1] http://www.ist-share.org/

M. Collard (Ed.): ODBIS 2005/2006, LNCS 4623, pp. 102–118, 2007.

instances [3]. Like most ontologies, the SHARE ontology (TBox and ABox) is stored as an external xml file (OWL-file) to disk. This approach, however, is inefficient for very large spatial ontologies that require loading the entire OWL file from disk into main memory for further processing.

In the context of non-spatial ontologies there have been approaches [4], [5] to distinguish the ontological model from the actual instances, which make use of a relational database system (RDBMS). In this way individual instances are stored as tuples in the database, and as a consequence only the required instances are read from the database and processed in memory. Despite the obvious gains from this approach, in SHARE ODS, we have observed significance performance problems in the spatial sub-ontology. This is due to the lack of efficient spatial query processing. The most important reason is that relational storage modelling is inefficient when dealing with space. Early attempts in this area focused on creating spatial database models and query languages, as well as on devising logic representations and algebras for reasoning about space. The emergence of the Semantic Web vision and related technologies, such as ontologies and semantic web services, has put Spatial Knowledge Representation under a whole new perspective.

To illustrate the problem, consider a large spatial ontology base storing objects (instances) at various locations. These objects have spatial attributes, such as x, y coordinates representing the object's location and the area it covers is represented as a minimum bounding rectangle. Apart from these spatial properties, each object refers to a concept of the ontology (TBox taxonomy) and consists of non-spatial aspects, such as the type of the object (e.g. building, hotel), height of the building, roof type, etc. Our goal is to answer queries that combine spatial with non-spatial (thematic) aspects over this database of objects effectively and to discard during the search process unnecessary objects from consideration.

In this paper, we focus on supporting the querying and management of large spatial ontologies. We propose to store the instances of the spatial sub-ontology using a spatial index structure (e.g. R-tree [6]). In this way we are able to support efficient query processing over large spatial ontologies. In addition, we are able to combine spatial query processing with reasoning mechanisms to speed up the process of inferring new knowledge. Our contributions can be summarized as follows. First, we address the problem of management of large spatial ontologies and we propose a hybrid approach that uses a spatial index structure (R-tree) as the underlying storage model. Second, a case-study using the SHARE system is presented showing how a spatial ontology can benefit from a spatial index structure. In addition, we present a series of experiments showing the performance gains.

The rest of the paper is organized as follows. Section 2 discusses related work. Section 3 presents the SHARE Ontology Data Service and motivates the need for spatial indexing. In Section 4 we show how we can index large spatial ontologies supporting efficient spatial query processing and present a case study using the SHARE system. The experimental results are presented in Section 5. Finally, Section 6 concludes the paper with directions for further work.

2   Background

The power of Geographical Information Systems (GIS) which integrate ontologies describing thematic aspects of entities has yet to be fully explored. An information system which can use ontology to capture spatial as well as non-spatial aspects has enormous potential in many application areas, such as national security and emergency response. A fast access to such ontology-enriched data, the volume of which is usually extremely large, requires the use of indexes, which can handle queries related to the location of the objects. In the remaining of this section we provide some background information related to ontology management and spatial query processing.

2.1   Ontology Management

In the context of non-spatial ontologies, an early attempt in [3] describes an environment for supporting very large ontologies. The system was created to manage ontologies of essentially unlimited size. The architecture of the system uses a relational database system as the storage model and describes different approaches to ontology management. In [5], the authors discuss DL reasoning over large ontologies (ABoxes) and present the KAON2. The system can decide knowledge base and concept satisfiability, compute the subsumption hierarchy, and answer conjunctive queries in which all variables are distinguished. The architecture of KAON2 is presented where the ontology API provides ontology manipulation services, such as adding and retrieving ontology axioms. The API fully supports OWL and the Semantic Web Rule Language (SWRL) at the syntactic level. ABox assertions are stored in a relational database (RDBMS). By mapping ontology entities to database tables, KAON2 is able to query the database on the fly during reasoning.

In the spatial domain, the majority of the work so far was related to the evolution of spatial databases, whose primary objective was to store spatial information and evolving geometries. Application of ontologies in GIS focuses on practical problems of defining a common vocabulary to describe the geospatial domain which can facilitate interoperability and limit data integration problems [7], [8]. On the Web, this use of ontology for better search and integration of geospatial data and applications is embodied in the Geospatial Semantic Web [9]. A system which provides Geographical Information Systems (GISs) with enhanced capabilities for supporting spatio-temporal reasoning is presented in [4].

Simultaneous to our study, Wessel and Moller [10] examine various methods to solve the map representation problem. However, their focus is on Description Logics reasoning using qualitative spatial information. Similar to our work the authors propose the use of an exterior component (called SBox, typically an R-tree [6]) combined with the rest of the ontology to answer spatio-thematic queries. Their hybrid approach uses both components in an interactive fashion. In addition they examine the materialization of spatial relationships and propose a graph structure (called RCC graph). Moreover, the authors decide not to represent the geometry of the map at all, but just exhaustively represent certain selected qualitative spatial aspects of the map, using a predefined qualitative spatial description vocabulary. This approach has essential drawbacks. Even though it is easy to compute such an ABox from the explicit geometry of a map, the resulting ABox is very large. Nevertheless, the size of the generated ABoxes may become a serious problem if bigger maps are considered. Typical maps gives rise to over 29 million role membership assertions! Since the RCC network is explicitly encoded in the ABox, the number of required role assertions is quadratic in the number of map objects. In addition, most spatial aspects cannot be handled in that way. For example, distance relations are very important for map queries, such as range queries and for that reason query processing is not efficient.

2.2   Spatial Query Processing

The problem of spatial indexing has motivated several research efforts. In this regard, the R-tree [6] is one of the most popular spatial index structures. For a comprehensive study on spatial index structures, see [11]. Each spatial data object in the R-tree is represented by a Minimum Bounding Rectangle (MBR). Leaf nodes in the R-tree contain entries of the form $(oid, rect)$ where oid is a pointer to the object in the database and $rect$ is the MBR of the object. Non-leaf nodes contain entries of the form $(ptr, rect)$ where ptr is a pointer to a child node in the R-tree and $rect$ is the MBR that covers all the MBRs in the child node.

For the following examples we use the R-tree of Figure 1, which indexes a set of points $\{a, b, ..., k\}$, assuming a capacity of three entries per node. Points that are close in space (e.g., a and b) are clustered in the same leaf node ($N3$), represented as a minimum bounding rectangle (MBR). Nodes are then recursively grouped together following the same principle until the top level, which consists of a single root. See [6] for more details on the R-tree construction.

R-trees (like most spatial access methods) were motivated by the need to efficiently process range queries, where the range usually corresponds to a rectangular window or a circular area around a query point. The R-tree answers the range query q (shaded area) in Figure 1 as follows. The root is first retrieved and the entries (e.g., $E1, E2$) that intersect the range are recursively searched because they may contain qualifying points. Nonintersecting entries (e.g., $E4$)

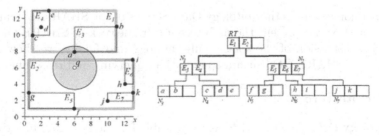

Fig. 1. Spatial Queries on R-trees

are skipped. Notice that for non-point data (e.g., lines, polygons), the R-tree provides just a filter step to prune non-qualifying objects. The output of this phase has to pass through a refinement step that examines the object representation to determine the actual result. The concept of filter and refinement steps applies to all spatial queries on non-point objects.

Besides range queries the *nearest neighbor* (NN) query retrieves the k ($k \geq 1$) data point(s) closest to a query point q. The R-tree NN algorithm proposed in [12] keeps a heap with the entries of the nodes visited so far. Initially, the heap contains the entries of the root sorted according to their minimum distance (*mindist*) from q. The entry with the minimum *mindist* in the heap ($E2$ in Figure 1) is expanded, i.e., it is removed from the heap and its children ($E5, E6$ and $E7$) are added together with their *mindist*. The next entry visited is $E1$ (its *mindist* is currently the minimum in the heap), followed by $E3$, where the actual 1-NN result (a) is found. The algorithm terminates, because the *mindist* of all entries in the heap is greater than the distance of a. The algorithm can be easily extended for the retrieval of k nearest neighbors (k-NN). Furthermore, it is optimal (it visits only the nodes necessary for obtaining the nearest neighbors) and incremental, i.e., it reports neighbors in ascending order of their distance to the query point, and can be applied when the number of nearest neighbors to be retrieved is unknown in advance.

3   The SHARE Ontology Data Service

The basis for our work is the SHARE Ontology Data Service (SHARE-ODS) [1]. SHARE-ODS combines multimedia semantic modeling and spatio-temporal modeling in a unified ontology. The main objective of the project SHARE is to develop a new type of advanced mobile service, called *Push-To-Share*, to support "mobile content sharing" by the participants of field operational teams, such as fire rescue forces. Push-To-Share is an innovative extension of the Push-To-Talk mobile technology and provides a new concept for simple ways of complex communication, combining an easy-to-use interface with a comfortable delivery of multimedia content. SHARE incorporates innovations in the area of multimodal interaction, robust speech interfaces, interactive digital maps, in conjunction with location-based services and intelligent information processing of multimedia data.

This Section discusses the Ontology Data Service of the SHARE system. More particularly, first we present the architectural framework of SHARE-ODS, followed by a discussion of the spatial sub-ontology and finally, we show several operations of SHARE-ODS such as population, querying and reasoning.

3.1   Architecture

The Ontology Data Service (ODS) is responsible for the semantic indexing and retrieval of the data in the Knowledge Base. More specifically, the various data (geographical, temporal, multimedia, operational) required for the operation of the overall architecture, are represented as ontology instances that are interconnected with semantic relations, providing an integrated view of the information needed to support the operation. The Ontology Data Service allows the querying of the Knowledge Base, so that the other services are able to retrieve not only the explicitly stated knowledge but also the implicit knowledge inferred by the reasoning engine.

The ODS operates as the back-end of the Data Server, supporting the functions of front-end data services like, for example, multimedia data retrieval and geographical annotation (Figure 2). Its main functionality is to allow the other Services to access populate and query the Knowledge Base. The functions of the ODS are available through a Web Service interface, so that they can be utilized by different software modules, which are implemented in different programming languages and situated in different network locations. In addition, the Ontology Data Service includes internal operations (consistency check, classification), which are responsible for detecting and correcting semantic discrepancies in the Knowledge Base. From the above discussion it is clear that efficient management of large ontologies is of major importance for the SHARE system.

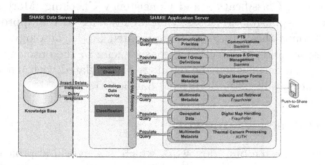

Fig. 2. General architecture of the Ontology Data Service

3.2   The Spatial Sub-ontology

The space conceptual model was designed taking into account the relationships that the map format provides, and its aim is to effectively model all the concepts related with geographical objects. The space conceptual model is represented by the spatial sub-ontology. The sub-ontology is broken down into two component sub-ontologies. The first one comprises abstract geographical concepts, their georeference, and the relationships between them. The second one includes actual features (buildings, streets, etc). Both SAR instances and geographical features represent their geo-references as relationships to the abstract geographical instances. Geographical meta-data describe the spatial properties of each entity, as well as the spatial relations among different entities. This information is crucial for constructing a semantic spatial context. The client application implementing the geographical data visualization is responsible for populating and updating the Knowledge Base with the appropriate spatial entities by utilizing specially predefined functions of the Web Service interface.

3.3 Operations

The Ontology Data Service allows the *population* of the ontology with the insertion of new instances, which are related to SaR operations, space or multimedia objects. The population process can be divided into two phases: the population that occurs during the initialization of the system and the population that occurs during the progress of a SaR operation. During initialization, the ontology is populated with static data (e.g. the geographical objects of the digital maps, the roster of the fire department) and setup data (e.g. the communication groups, the available communication devices). On the other hand, during operation time the ontology is populated with dynamic data (e.g. event logging, formation of new sections, moving objects).

Furthermore, the Ontology Data Service allows the *querying* of the stored knowledge. Queries are expressed in RDQL, in order to take advantage of the graph-like structure of the ontology. More specifically, the queries can impose constraints on the property values, as well as on the relations of instances. This way a query graph is created which has to be matched with the actual ontology graph.

Besides population and querying, the Ontology Data Service supports two *reasoning* services: Classification and Consistency Checking. More specifically, classification is responsible for classifying an instance to the appropriate class taking into account the knowledge incorporated in the ontology. Consistency checking is responsible for detecting inconsistencies in the ontology knowledge. Inconsistencies can occur when the ontology is populated with inaccurate data or when an unacceptable situation (fact) has occurred.

4 The Proposed Framework

In this section we sketch our framework which is a hybrid approach extending the classical R-tree by using ontologies. The main difference to the R-tree is the additional storage of non-spatial annotation, i.e. each leaf entry is augmented with non-spatial (thematic) information. As an application scenario, we consider the incorporation of an R-tree inside SHARE-ODS. More specifically subsection 4.1 motivates the need for spatial query processing, subsection 4.2 presents the process of the index construction and finally in subsection 4.3 we discuss query processing using the SHARE Ontology Data Service.

4.1 Motivation

In this Section we define two cases, which require efficient support of spatial query processing inside SHARE-ODS. The first case concerns spatial query processing in a dynamically changing environment, i.e. during a SaR operation, whereas the second case deals with static spatial entities, such as entities populated in the initialization stage. We start with two commonly used spatial query types, namely range and nearest neighbour queries, in order to illustrate the problem.

Query 1. *"Find all hospitals in a particular area (range) which are appropriate for landing a helicopter"*. First of all, during query processing only hospitals are retrieved that lies in the given area, in contrast to Description Logics systems or spatial ontology bases (such as the current SHARE ontology) which stores spatial related data but quantitative information can not be supported. Thereafter, a refinement is required to ensure that the object refers to a hospital and there is a helicopter landing facility for an emergency landing which are of appropriate length and have sufficient fire-fighting crews and equipment. In order to find this information, we may use TBox reasoning.

Query 2. *"Find the nearest hospitals, according to my current location, which is appropriate for landing a helicopter"*. Again, during query processing we have to check for a helicopter landing facility but for this query the objects are sorted based on their distance to the current position. Objects that are far away are immediately discarded while objects are refined in order to identify whether they are hospitals with a helicopter landing facility.

Besides these two queries on static data, a user of the SHARE system may also pose a query on the dynamic changing data. Consider as an example that we store in the ontology the sections and sub-sections defined by the Officer in Charge (see [1], [2] for more details). Each section (sub-section) is assigned to a B-Level Officer and is represented as a spatial region (area). Assuming a querying operation that requests the B-Level Officers, which are responsible for sections: (1) "Find all B-Level Officers and corresponding sections in a particular area." or (2) "Find the B-Level Officer who is closest to an accident (e.g. fire)".

The first query retrieves all B-Level Officers inside a particular range. The second query retrieves the nearest B-Level Officer to a specific point. Unfortunately, traditional ontology-based approaches are unable to answer effectively these types of spatial queries, resulting in a high processing time. These queries are either posed directly from an ODS client or they are part of a longer chain of reasoning steps, involving various concepts and relations in the SHARE ontology.

4.2   Index Construction

In this sub-section we propose to support SHARE-ODS using a disk-resident R-tree to store spatially related instances and at the same time we propose the use of the OWL file for non-spatial instances. In this way, individual non-spatial instances are stored in the OWL file, while spatial instances are stored in the R-tree and as a consequence only the required instances are read from the disk and processed in memory. The spatial information that is involved in our R-tree based framework relates to instances (objects) of the ontology which refer to spatial concepts. These instances are stored using the R-tree as a physical storage model. Note that for large non-spatial sub-ontologies a back-end RDBMS may be used to store non-spatial instances as tuples in the database. However, management of non-spatial ontologies is beyond the scope of this paper. In the remaining of this section we present the process of the index construction.

In our approach the R-tree is built by storing the ontological annotation of the spatial objects. Therefore we keep in the leaves of the R-tree an identifier (ID) which associates the object information with instances of the ontology.

More specifically, a non-leaf node of the R-tree contains entries of the form $(child - pointer, MBR)$ where $child - pointer$ is the address of a child node in the R-tree, and MBR is the minimum bounding rectangle of all rectangles which are entries in that child node. A leaf node contains entries of the form $(MBR, Ontology - ID)$ where MBR is the enclosing rectangle of that spatial object and $Ontology - ID$ is an identifier that refers to instances of the ontology.

We first describe how to insert a new entry in the R-tree. Given a new entry (i.e. object), the insertion algorithm decides in which node the entry should be inserted based on spatial criteria, such as [13], minimizing the following penalty metrics: (i) the area, (ii) the perimeter of each MBR, (iii) the overlap between two MBRs in the same node, and (iv) the distance between the centroid of an MBR. As discussed in [13], minimization of these metrics decreases the probability that an MBR intersects a query region.

During the insertion, at each level of the tree the algorithm chooses the branch to follow in a greedy manner. Assume we insert a new object into the tree. At the root level, the algorithm chooses the entry whose MBR needs the least enlargement to cover the new entry. Then, at the next level, the algorithm chooses the entry whose MBR enlargement leads to the smallest overlap increase among the sibling entries in the node. Note that different metrics are considered at different levels of the tree structure. If the leaf node reached the new entry is inserted and the MBR of the parent node is tested if it covers the new entry and if necessary it is enlarged. If the parent MBR need to enlarge this modification is propagated to upper levels, in order to enlarge also those MBRs, if necessary. In the leaves of the R-tree we store objects which corresponds to instances of ontology concepts, e.g. hotel, park, house.

Let as consider that the spatial sub-ontology consists of buildings associated with a location. Then, the R-tree corresponds to a "map" where each building (e.g. hospitals) is represented as a point. Other ontological information such as type of the object (e.g. building), its height, roof type, etc. are stored in the owl file (see Figure 3). This approach enables the efficient processing of advanced spatial queries such as range and nearest neighbor queries based on the position of the buildings, while also ontological constrains are evaluated.

In Figure 3, the process of distinguishing between spatial and non-spatial characteristics is shown. Instances referring to the spatial sub-ontology are additionally

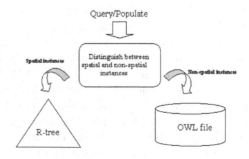

Fig. 3. Storing the instances

indexed by the R-tree in order to speed up the query processing, whereas instances referring to other sub-components of the ontology (e.g. multimedia or operational sub-ontologies) are stored only in the OWL file. Note that, this process happens inside the Ontology Data Service and is application specific, i.e. the knowledge of an expert is required to mark the spatial characteristics of the ontology. The ontological model is kept in main memory (due to its relatively small size) as it is requested very often.

4.3 Query Processing

In this Section we discuss query processing using our proposed framework. Let us assume that our database stores objects (instances which refer to spatial concepts) at various locations. These objects have spatial attributes, such as x, y coordinates representing the object's location and the area it covers is represented as a minimum bounding rectangle. Apart from these spatial properties each object has some ontological information, referring to concepts of the TBox such as the type of the object (e.g. building), its height, roof type, etc. Our goal is to answer queries referring to spatial and/or ontological information over this database of objects effectively and to discard during the search process unnecessary objects from consideration.

Our framework can execute queries that combine both the ontology and the R-tree in longer chains of reasoning steps. In such cases, the R-tree queries are used to reduce the complexity of the RDQL statements. We show in more detail this process using our hybrid approach. For this reason, we use the two query types of the previous section.

Range and Nearest Neighbor Queries

Our R-tree based framework answers a range query q (shaded area) in Figure 1 (cf. section 2.2) as follows. We assume that the query consists of (1) spatial parts (i.e. the query point q and a range) as well as non-spatial parts (i.e. hospitals with helicopter landing facility). In addition we show how to process k nearest neighbor queries enhanced with non-spatial query parts.

Example. (*Range Query*) Consider as an example that we are interested in hospitals appropriate for landing a helicopter inside a specified region (cf. section 2.2). The R-tree is used as a filter step to prune non-qualifying objects, i.e. buildings outside the specified region. The output of this phase has to pass through the non-spatial ontology to determine the objects with the appropriate roof type. Finally, the actual result is presented to the user (i.e. highlight the buildings on the map).

More specifically, the algorithm for processing range queries using our framework is as follows. The root is first retrieved and the entries (e.g., $E1, E2$) that intersect the range are recursively searched. Nonintersecting entries (e.g., $E4$) are skipped. The output of this phase has to pass through a refinement step that evaluates non-spatial (e.g. thematic) query parts to determine the actual result.

Example.(*Nearest Neighbor Query*) Assume we are interested in the nearest hospital appropriate for landing a helicopter. We execute an incremental k nearest neighbor query (with unknown k) to obtain a ranking of the nearest buildings according to the user's current location. This means that the first nearest neighbor is retrieved and tested against the non-spatial query part, i.e. if the object corresponds to a hospital and has the appropriate roof type. If the retrieved object does not correspond to the specification, the second nearest neighbor is retrieved and we continue until we have found a hospital with appropriate roof type.

More particularly, a nearest neighbor (NN) query which retrieves the k ($k \geq 1$) data point(s) closest to a query point q with non-spatial query parts is executed using our framework in the following way. Initially, the heap contains the entries of the root sorted according to their distance (*dist*) from q. The entry in the heap with the minimum dist is retrieved and if the entry is not an object, the entry is expanded, i.e., it is removed from the heap and its children are added. If the entry belongs to a leaf node, the ontology instance is accessed using the associated ontology ID after the non-spatial query part is evaluated by the reasoner. If the non-spatial specification holds the instance is returned as the nearest neighbor. Else, the second nearest neighbor is retrieved i.e. the next leaf entry whose *dist* is currently the minimum in the heap. We continue until we have found k object which meets our spatial and/or non-spatial requirements.

Note that, for the above queries the R-tree is used to speed-up the query processing. Therefore we are able to retrieve only a small fraction of the actual dataset (ABox) and organize the spatial entities in a more appropriate way.

5   Experimental Evaluation

For the purpose of the experiments, we used SHARE-ODS [1], [2] for generating the dataset. As a scenario for the experiments we consider the buildings described in the spatial sub-ontology. In our experiments, the dataset contains buildings with varied cardinalities, ranging from 100 points to 10,000 points. In the first set of experiments we study the scalability of the original SHARE-ODS and show that this approach has serious performance shortcomings. In the second set of experiments, we examine the query performance with the dataset cardinality for spatial range queries and nearest neighbor queries (pre-computed and dynamic). More specifically, we examine the performance degradation in the case of increasing dataset cardinality and we report the running time as a function of the number of instances. In our third experiment we examine the more complex case of combining spatial query processing with the rest ontology. We study the influence of the R-tree on the performance and examine the scalability with respect to the query.

All these experiments use an R-tree indexing 2-dimensional points corresponding to static landmarks (e.g. buildings), which is built during the initialization process. In the last experiment we examine the performance of the R-tree in case of dynamically changing spatial information corresponding to the operational spatial sub-ontology. In this case regions are inserted in the R-tree that corresponds to the areas that are assigned to a B-Level Officer during an operation. For the R-tree implementation we use the XXL library [14].

5.1   Shortcomings of the Original Ontology

In this subsection we are particularly interested in the impact of the current SHARE-ODS implementation. We examine the performance by varying the number of instances (in our case 2-dimensional points) from 100 to 1,000. Note that, a building on a 2-dimensional map is covering a particular area. This area is represented in SHARE-ODS as a closed line. On the other hand, a very common approach used by almost all maps is to represent a building as a 2-dimensional point. To support efficient query processing, a building in SHARE-ODS is additional represented as a point characterized by the latitude and the longitude (data properties). In the original ontology to support nearest neighbor query each building has eight object properties corresponding to the eight closest buildings in each direction (e.g. south, west, etc.), which in turn increases the size of the OWL file. We report the CPU time (in msec) required for the ODS population.

Figure 4 shows the CPU time needed to load the dataset (OWL file) from the disc. In addition we report the time for saving the OWL file to disc. For both cases we observed a high increase in the CPU time for large datasets (above 900 instances).

5.2   Query Processing for Spatial Ontologies

In the second set of experiments we study the performance of two spatial query types, namely range queries and nearest neighbor queries. Additionally, we distinguish between the pre-computed nearest neighbor and the dynamic case. The former, is used for comparison using the R-tree.

In our running example, the points stored in the R-tree correspond to the buildings represented in the spatial sub-ontology. Actually, the latitude and the longitude that are data properties of the building are stored in the R-tree. In the first experiment, we vary the number of buildings and we are interested to find the buildings that lay in a particular area.

In Figure 5, we report the CPU time needed for answering a range query with constant cardinality for different number of instances. We vary the number of instances between 100 and 10,000. For the OWL file we observed a high increase in the CPU time, while for the R-tree the CPU time remains almost constant.

In the following experiment we are interested to find the nearest building based on a particular direction. As already mentioned, in the original approach the nearest neighbors are pre-calculated and stored in the OWL file as object properties of a building. In contrast to the original case, the R-tree supports such nearest neighbor queries dynamically and the nearest neighbor is calculated real time with respect to the preferred direction. In addition, we examine the dynamic case of nearest neighbor query. We are interested to find the nearest building to a random point on the map. This means that the query point is not necessary a

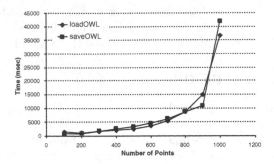

Fig. 4. Performance shortcomings

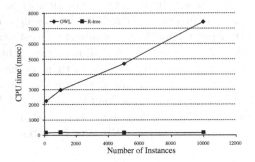

Fig. 5. Spatial Range Query

building. The original approach does not support efficiently this query since the nearest neighbor of a random point cannot be pre-calculated and stored in the OWL file.

Figure 6a shows the CPU time needed to answer a nearest neighbor query with respect to the number of points inserted in the ontology. Again, for the OWL file we observed a high increase in the CPU time, and more specifically when the dataset cardinality exceeds a certain threshold. For the R-tree the CPU time remains almost constant. Figure 6b depicts the CPU time needed for retrieving the nearest neighbor from an arbitrary query point. As already mentioned, this query cannot be pre-computed and cannot be computed efficiently when using the OWL file. The number of building is varied between 100 and 10,000 instances and we measure the CPU time. We observe that the required CPU time increases very slowly with increasing number of instaces.

5.3   Combining Spatial Query Processing with the Rest of the Ontology

In this subsection we investigate the performance of our approach under the assumption that the query is answered using both the OWL file and the R-tree. Such an example is the query "Find which buildings in a particular area (range) are appropriate for landing a helicopter". The location of the building is a spatial

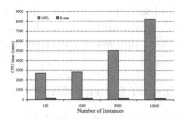 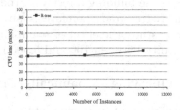

(a) Nearest Neighbor (pre-computed in OWL) (b) Dynamic Nearest Neighbor Query

Fig. 6. Dynamic vs. pre-computed Nearest Neighbor

attribute and kept in the R-tree. The data property of a building that indicates if a helicopter is capable to land on a building is a non-spatial attribute and is kept in the OWL file.

In this example the R-tree is used as a filter to simplify the RDQL statement. In a first step, all buildings that lie in the particular area are retrieved. The building identifier is also stored in the R-tree as a label of each point. In a second step, the buildings are retrieved from the OWL file according to the identifier and buildings that are not suitable for a helicopter are discarded from the result set.

In the following experiment we compare the combined approach in contrast to the performance of the RDQL statement of the original approach. Figure 7 illustrates the effect of the number of instances on a query that can be answered by the OWL file and additionally by the combination of the OWL file and the R-tree. As expected, using the combined approach is superior to the original approach, which uses only the OWL file. Especially when the number of instances increases, the gain of our approach increases rapidly. This is due to the fact that the RDQL query is simplified through a filtering step using the R-tree, which in turn decreases the time, needed for the query processing. Moreover, the combined approach avoids the retrieving of points based on the data properties of an object, i.e. the latitude of the point corresponding to the building, but

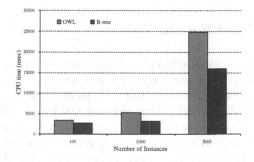

Fig. 7. Combined Query

accesses the building directly by the building's identifier. The identifier is stored in the R-tree and therefore is able to reduce significantly the CPU time. In order to study the effect of scalability for our point dataset, we vary the dataset cardinality between 100 and 5,000 instances.

5.4   Querying Dynamically-Changing Spatial Information

In this experiment we simulate a rescue operation by inserting and deleting region that are assigned to a B-Level Officer (cf. section 3.1). The B-Level Officer's identifier is stored in the R-tree and therefore is able to reduce significantly the CPU time.

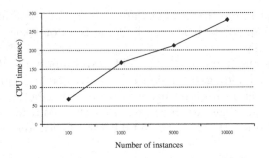

Fig. 8. Dynamic R-tree

Figure 8 depicts the CPU time needed for retrieving the B-Level Officer of the nearest region to an arbitrary query point. The total number of inserted region instances is varied between 100 and 10,000. To simulate the process of a Search and Rescue operation we randomly delete some regions and reinsert other regions. The general performance of an R-tree is influenced by deletions and we encounter this fact in our experiments. We observe that the required CPU time increases very slowly when the number of instances increases rapidly. Despite the deletions required for dynamically changing spatial information the R-tree performs well in terms of CPU time for answering spatial queries.

6   Conclusions and Future Work

We have proposed a method for efficient management of large spatial ontologies, which combines a typical OWL ontology with an R-tree for indexing spatial entities. The performance evaluation shows the superiority of our proposed technique compared to the original approach, using only the OWL file. Using the proposed approach, we are able to support efficient query processing over large spatial ontologies and integrate it in a larger chain of reasoning steps. In addition we present a case study for emergency teams during Search and Rescue (SaR) operations showing how the SHARE Ontology Data Service can benefit from a spatial index, which is integrated inside the SHARE system.

As future work we plan to extend this work to several directions. First of all, we indent to investigate more complex spatial query operators, such as spatial joins combining thematic aspects within our framework. Second, the integration of spatio-temporal indexing into ontologies, which represent both concepts of space and time is of major importance. Finally, we aim to design an index structure that keeps class membership information in the nodes of the tree. During query processing nodes are discarded by testing the thematic part of the query against the characteristics of the nodes. By separating the ontological model (TBox) from the actual instances (ABox) we are moving towards efficient management of very large spatial knowledge bases while at the same time query processing would benefit from this approach.

Acknowledgments

The authors wish to acknowledge the support of the EC-funded project SHARE (contract no. FP6-IST-004218) to the work reported in this paper.

References

1. Konstantopoulos, S., Paliouras, G., Chantzinotas, S.: Share-ods: An ontology data service for search and rescue operations. In: Antoniou, G., Potamias, G., Spyropoulos, C., Plexousakis, D. (eds.) SETN 2006. LNCS (LNAI), vol. 3955, pp. 525–528. Springer, Heidelberg (2006)
2. Konstantopoulos, S., Paliouras, G., Chantzinotas, S.: Share-ods: An ontology data service for search and rescue operations. In: Technical Report DEMO-2006-1, NCSR 'Demokritos', Athens (2006)
3. Stoffel, K., Taylor, M.G., Hendler, J.A.: Efficient management of very large ontologies. In: American Association for Artificial Intelligence Conference (AAAI), pp. 442–447 (1997)
4. Raffaeta, A., Turini, F., Renso, C.: Enhancing giss for spatio-temporal reasoning. In: ACM International Symposium on Geographic Information Systems (ACM-GIS), pp. 42–48. ACM Press, New York (2002)
5. Motik, B., Sattler, U.: Practical dl reasoning over large aboxes with kaon2. In: Submitted for publication (2006), http://www.fzi.de/ipe/eng/publikationen.php
6. Guttman, A.: R-trees: A dynamic index structure for spatial searching. In: ACM SIGMOD International Conference on Management of Data (SIGMOD), pp. 47–57. ACM Press, New York (1984)
7. Agarwal, P.: Ontological considerations in giscience. International Journal of Geographical Information Science 19(5), 501–536 (2005)
8. Fonseca, F.T., Egenhofer, M.J., Agouris, P., Câmara, G.: Using ontologies for integrated geographical information systems. Transactions in Geographic Information Systems 6(3) (2002)
9. Egenhofer, M.J.: Toward the semantic geospatial web. In: ACM International Symposium on Geographic Information Systems (ACM-GIS), pp. 1–4. ACM Press, New York (2002)
10. Wessel, M., Möller, R.: A flexible dl-based architecture for deductive information systems. In: IJCAR Workshop on Empirically Successful Computerized Reasoning (ESCoR), pp. 92–111 (2006)

11. Gaede, V., Günther, O.: Multidimensional access methods. ACM Computing Surveys 30(2), 170–231 (1998)
12. Hjaltason, G.R., Samet, H.: Distance browsing in spatial databases. ACM Transactions on Database Systems 24(2), 265–318 (1999)
13. Beckmann, N., Kriegel, H.P., Schneider, R., Seeger, B.: The r*-tree: An efficient and robust access method for points and rectangles. In: ACM SIGMOD International Conference on Management of Data (SIGMOD), pp. 322–331. ACM Press, New York (1990)
14. den Bercken, J.V., Blohsfeld, B., Dittrich, J.P., Krämer, J., Schäfer, T., Schneider, M., Seeger, B.: Xxl - a library approach to supporting efficient implementations of advanced database queries. In: International Conference on Very Large Data Bases (VLDB), pp. 39–48 (2001)

Knowledge Extraction Using a Conceptual Information System (ExCIS)

Laurent Brisson

Laboratoire I3S - Université de Nice, 06903 Sophia-Antipolis, France
brisson@i3s.unice.fr

Abstract. It is a well known fact that the data mining process can generate thousands of patterns from data. Various measures exist for evaluating and ranking these discovered patterns but often they don't consider user subjective interest. We propose an ontology-based data-mining methodology called ExCIS (Extraction using a Conceptual Information System) for integrating expert prior knowledge in a data-mining process. Its originality is to build a specific Conceptual Information System related to the application domain in order to improve datasets preparation and results interpretation. This paper focus on our ontological choices and an interestingness measure IMAK which evaluates patterns considering expert knowledge.

1 Introduction

One important challenge in data mining is to extract interesting knowledge and useful information for expert users. Numerous works focused on indexes that measure the interestingness of a mined pattern [5,9]. They generally distinguished objective and subjective interest. Silberschatz and Tuzhilin [14] proposed a method to define unexpectedness and actionability via *belief systems* while Liu [9] developed a method that use *user expectations.*

In most data mining projects, prior knowledge is implicit or is not organized as a structured conceptual system. ExCIS is dedicated to data mining situations where the expert knowledge is crucial for the interpretation of mined patterns. In this approach, an application ontology is built by analyzing existing databases with collaboration of expert users who play a central role. The main objective in ExCIS is to propose a framework in which the extraction process makes use of a well-formed conceptual information system (CIS) for improving the quality of mined knowledge. We consider the paradigm of CIS as defined by Stumme [18]: a relationnal database together with conceptual hierarchies. The CIS provides an useful structure for further mining tasks.

An ontology is a logical theory accounting for the intended meaning of a formal vocabulary, i.e. its ontological commitment to a particular conceptualization of the world [4]. Extracting ontological structures from data is very similar to processes of retrieving a conceptual schema from legacy databases [6]. They are based on the assumption that sufficient knowledge is stored in databases in order to construct the ontology.. They generally apply a matching between ontological

M. Collard (Ed.): ODBIS 2005/2006, LNCS 4623, pp. 119–134, 2007.

concepts and relational tables such that the ontology extracted is very close to the conceptual database schema.

In ExCIS, the ontology provides a conceptual representation of the application domain by analyzing the existing operational databases. ExCIS main characteristics are:

- Prior knowledge conceptualization: the CIS is specially designed for data mining tasks
- Adaptation of the CRISP-DM [2] methodology with CIS based preparation of data sets to be mined, CIS based post processing of mined knowledge in order to extract surprising and/or actionable knowledge and an incremental evolution of the expert knowledge stored in the CIS.

Our project deals with data from the 'family' branch of the French national health care system. The issue we address is to improve relationships between beneficiaries and the CAF organism. In this case study, we had two sources of information: a database storing data on beneficiaries and expert users aware of the business processes, behaviors and habits in the organism.

The topic of this paper is the use of ontologies for data mining. Our goal is to enhance data mining tasks and to extract interesting patterns according user's knowledge. The novelty of ExCIS methodology lies in the creation of a CIS in order to compare knowledge and extracted patterns. We use an ontology based approach for unexpected and actionable patterns extraction while works on interestingness measures deals with templates [9] or beliefs [14]. Furthermore, using user's knowledge in actionable patterns extraction differs from Piatetsky-Shapiro [13] or Silberschatz [15] approaches.

The paper is organized as follows. Section 2 presents related works. Section 3 gives an overview of the ExCIS approach. Section 4 describes the underlying conceptual structures of the ontology. In Section 5, we give a detailed description of CIS construction. Section 6 focus on knowledge database construction and interesting patterns extraction. Section 7 presents experiments results. Section 8 concludes the paper.

2   Related Works

2.1   Interestingness Measures

Numerous works focused on indexes that measure the interestingness of a mined pattern [5,9,10]. They generally distinguished objective and subjective interest. Among these indexes there are quantitative measures of objective interestingness such as confidence, coverage, lift, success rate while unexpectedness and actionability are proposed for subjective criteria. Since our work deals with user interestingness, we focus this state of the art on the former. According to the actionability criteria, a model is interesting if the user can start some action depending on it [15]. On the other hand, unexpected models are considered interesting since they contradict user expectations which depend on his beliefs.

User expectations is a method developed by Liu [9]. The first approach neither dealt with unexpectedness nor actionability. User had to specify a set of patterns according to his previous knowledge and intuitive feelings. Patterns had to be expressed in the same way that mined patterns. Then Liu defined a fuzzy algorithm which matches these patterns. In order to find actionable patterns, the user has to specify all actions that he could take. Then, for each action he specifies the situation under which he is likely to run the action. Finally, the system matches each discovered pattern against the patterns specified by the user using a fuzzy matching technique.

Silberschatz and Tuzhilin [14] proposed a method to define unexpectedness via belief systems. In this approach, there are two kinds of beliefs: soft beliefs that the user is willing to change if new patterns are discovered and hard beliefs which are constraints that cannot be changed with new discovered knowledge. Consequently this approach assumes that we can believe in some statements only partially. That's why some degree or confidence factor is assigned to each belief. A pattern is said to be interesting relatively to some belief system if it 'affects' this system, and the more it 'affects' it, the more interesting it is. However, interestingness of a pattern depends also on the kind of belief.

2.2 Databases and Ontologies

Ontologies provide a formal support to express beliefs and prior knowledge on a domain. Domain ontologies are not always available; they have to be built specially by querying expert users or by analyzing existing data. Extracting ontological structures from data is very similar to the process of retrieving a conceptual schema from legacy databases. Different methods [7,6,17] were proposed. They are based on the assumption that sufficient knowledge is stored in databases for producing an intelligent guide for ontology construction. They generally apply a matching between ontological concepts and relational tables such that the ontology extracted is very close to the conceptual database schema.

2.3 Ontologies and Data Mining

For the last ten years, ontologies have been extensively used for knowledge representation and analysis mainly in two domains: Bioinformatics and web content management. Biological knowledge is nowadays most often represented in 'bio-ontologies' that are formal representations of knowledge areas in which the essential terms are combined with structuring rules that describe relationships between the terms. Bio-ontologies are constructed according to textual descriptions of biological activities. One of the most popular bio-ontology is *Gene Ontology*[1] that contains more than 18 thousands terms. It describes the molecular function of a gene product, the biological process in which the gene product participates, and the cellular component where the gene product can be found. Results of data mining processes can then be linked to structured knowledge

---

[1] http://www.geneontology.org/

within bio-ontologies in order to explicit discovered knowledge, for instance to identify biological functions of genes within a cluster. Interesting surveys of ontologies usage for bio-informatics can be found in [1,16]. A successful project of data mining application using bio-ontologies is described in [19].

In the domain of web content management, OWL (Ontology Web Language)[2] is a Semantic Web standard that provides a framework for the management, the integration, the sharing and the reuse of data on the Web. Semantic Web aims at the sharing and processing of web data by automated tools as well as by people. It can be used to explicitly represent the meaning of terms in vocabularies and the relationships between those terms, i.e. an ontology. Web ontologies can be used to enrich and explain extracted patterns in many knowledge discovery applications to web such as web usage profiling [3] for instance.

3   Overview of the ExCIS Approach

ExCIS integrates prior knowledge all along the mining process: the first step structures and organizes the knowledge in the CIS and further steps exploit it and enrich it too.

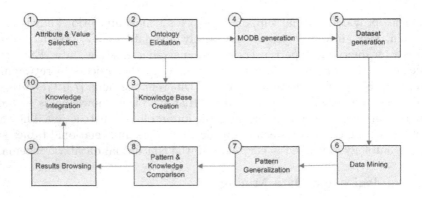

Fig. 1. ExCIS Process

Figure 1 describes ExCIS process from attribute selection to extraction of interesting patterns. Figure 2 describe information flow in ExCIS approach. On each arrow a number refers to a subprocess in figure 1. In this paper, section 4 describe subprocesses 1 to 3 while section 6 describe subprocess 8.

The global ExCIS process presented in theses figures shows:

– The CIS construction where:
   • The ontology is extracted by analyzing original databases and by interacting with expert users.

---

[2] http://www.w3.org/TR/owl-ref/

- The knowledge base, set of factual informations, is obtained in a first step from dialogs with expert users.
- The new generic Mining Oriented Database (MODB) is built. It contains data cleaned and prepared using domain knowledge.
- The pre-processing step where specific datasets may be built for specific mining tasks.
- The standard mining step which extracts patterns from these datasets.
- The post-processing step where discovered patterns may be interpreted and/or filtered according to both prior knowledge stored in the CIS and individual user attempt.

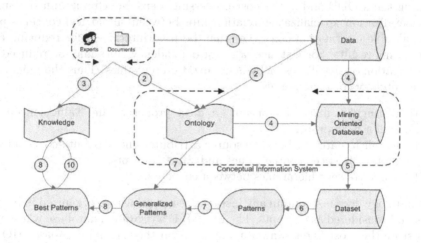

Fig. 2. Information flow

In this paper we call "patterns" a set of itemsets. Technicaly, we use the CLOSE algorithm [12] to extract association rules (one itemset for antecedent and another one for consequent).

The MODB is said to be generic since it will be used as a kind of basic data repository from which any task-specific dataset may be generated. We call MODB a relationnal database whose attributes and values are concepts of the ontology we defined. The underlying idea in the CIS is to build structures which will provide more flexibility not only for pre-processing the data to be mined, but for filtering and interpreting discovered patterns in a post-processing step. Hierarchical structures and generalization/specialization links between ontological concepts play a central role to allow reducing the volume of extracted patterns and to provide a tool for interpreting results obtained by clustering algorithms.

For numerical or categorical data, they provide different granularity levels which are useful in the pre-processing and the post-processing steps.

4   Conceptual Structures of the Ontology

4.1   Ontology

In ExCIS the ontology is an essential means both for improving data mining processes and for interpreting data mining results. It's an *application ontology* as defined by Guarino [4], ie. an ontology which describe concepts depending both on a particular domain (family branch of the french health care system in our application) and task (data mining in ExCIS methodology). The ontology is defined by a set of concepts and relationships among them which are discovered by analyzing existing data. It provides support both in the pre-processing step for building the MODB and in the post-processing steps for refining mined results.

Generalization/specialization relationships between ontological concepts provide valuable information since they may be used intensively for reducing and interpreting results. For instance, a set of dependency rules may be reduced by generalization on attributes or by generalization on values. Thus the guidelines in the ontology construction are:

- To distinguish attribute-concept (a data property) and value-concept (a value of a data property).
- To establish matching between source attributes and attribute-concepts and a matching between source values and value-concepts.
- To define concept hierarchies between concepts.

This ontology does not contain any instances since values are organized in hierarchies and considered as concepts. The MODB is a relational database whose role is to store the most fine-grain data elicited from the original database. MODB attributes are those which are identified as relevant for the data mining task and MODB tuples are composed of the most fine-grain values.

4.2   Ontology Relationships

A relationship is an oriented link between two concepts. In ExCIS there are two different kinds of concepts (see figure 3) and we distinguish relationships between concepts of the same hierarchy and concepts of different hierarchies.

Relationships from an attribute-concept toward a value-concept are forbidden since the relationship "is value of" has no meaning in this situation. There exist five different relationships between concepts (see Table 1). Numbers in this table refer to relationships in figure 4(a), 4(b) and 5. Among all the relationships, we can set up 3 different categories:

Relationships between value-concepts. Generalization or specialization relationships between value-concepts (see relationship 5 figure 5) are useful in order to generalize patterns during the post-processing step. Furthermore, relationships between two value concepts of *the same hierarchy* are essential since they allow to select data granularity in datasets generated from the MODB (see relationship 3 figure 4).

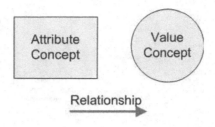

Fig. 3. Representation of concept and relationship

Table 1. Concept relationships

Concept	Within the same hierarchy		Between different hierarchies	
	Attribute	Value	Attribute	Value
Attribute	1 genls			
Value	2 valueOf	3 genls	4 valueOf	5 relationWith

Relationships between attribute-concepts. Generalization or specialization relationships between attribute-concepts are useful in order to generalize models during the post-processing step.

Relationships between two concrete attribute-concepts of the same hierarchy are specific because they have to be checked during datasets generation: indeed these attributes cannot be in the same dataset to avoid redundancy.

ExCIS method forbids relationships between attribute-concepts of different hierarchies because attribute-concepts which are semantically close have to be located together in the same hierarchy (see relationship 1 figures 4,5).

Relationships between value-concepts and attribute-concepts. These relationships are essential in order to build data or to provide different semantic views during the post-processing step. For instance, "98001" is both a "Home Location" and a "Zip Code" (see relationships 2,4 figure 5). If concepts are semantically close they must be in the same hierarchy and if they are slightly different they can be into two different hierarchies.

5   Conceptual Information System Construction

ExCIS differs from CRISP-DM mainly in the data preparation step. In this step CRISP-DM describes 5 tasks: select, clean, construct, integrate and format data. Selection and format are identical in both methods but in ExCIS cleaning, construction and integration are improved in order to elicitate the ontological concepts and to build the MODB.

Let A the set of source database attributes, C the set of ontology concepts and C_z the set of concepts associated to an attribute $z \in A$. C is defined by $\bigcup_{z \in A} C_z$.

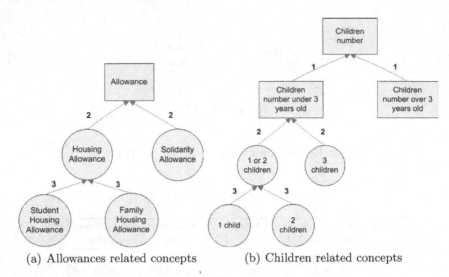

(a) Allowances related concepts   (b) Children related concepts

Fig. 4. Concept Hierarchies

5.1 Scope Definition and Source Attribute Selection

First steps of ExCIS method are related to the Business Understanding and the Data Understanding steps of CRISP DM method. They need an important interaction with expert users.

1. Determine objectives: in our case study, objectives are to improve "relationships with beneficiaries".
2. Define themes: analysis of data allow to gather them into semantic sets called themes. For example we create 3 themes: Allowance beneficiaries profiles, contacts (by phone, by mail, in the agency, ...) and events (holidays, school starts, birth, wedding, ...).
3. For each theme select a set of source attributes with experts users.

5.2 Data Analysis and Attribute-Concept Elicitation

4. For each selected attribute z:
   5. Examine name and description in order to:
   – Associate n concepts to the attribute.
   – Into C, clean homonyms (different concepts with same name), synonyms (same concepts with different names like age and date of birth) and useless attributes according the objectives.
   6. Examine values (distribution, missing values, duplicates values, ...) in order to:
   – Refine C_z (add or delete concepts) according to information collected in step 6.

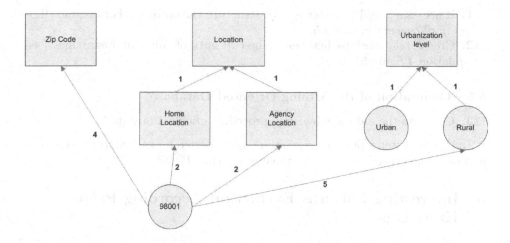

Fig. 5. Location related concepts

- Clean again homonyms, synonyms and useless attributes. For example by analyzing values we realized that 'allowances' was in fact 2 homonyms concepts. Thus we created the 'allowance amount' concept and the 'allowance beneficiary' concept.
7. For each concept associated to z create the method which generates value-concepts.

In the step 7, if the attribute-concept doesn't exist we have to create a 4 fields record table. These fields are the attribute associated to the concept, the name of the attribute table in source database, the attribute domain value and the reference to the procedure which may generate value-concepts. There is only one procedure for record in the table. A domain value can be a distinct value or a regular expression and is the input of the procedure. Procedure output provides references to value-concepts. The procedure might be an SQL request (SELECT or specific computation) or an external program (script, shell, C, . . .). However, if the attribute-concept already exists we just have to add a record in the table and create a new procedure.

5.3   Value-Concept Elicitation

At this point, all of the methods to generate value-concepts are created.

8. Give a name to each value-concept.
9. Clean homonyms and synonyms among value-concepts.

5.4   Ontology Structuration

10. Identify generalization relationships among value-concepts (see figure 4(a)).

11. If necessary, add new concepts to structure the ontology. For instance 'Location' concept in figure 5.
12. Create relationships between value-concepts of different hierarchies (see relation 4 figure 5).

5.5   Generation of the Mining Oriented Database

13. Generate the database by using procedures defined in step 7.

In this final step a program reads the tables created for each attribute-concept and calls the procedures in order to generate the MODB.

6   Interesting Patterns Extraction According Prior Knowledge

6.1   Knowledge Properties

We chose to express knowledge like "if ... then ..." rules in order to simplify comparison with extracted association rules. Each knowledge have some essential properties to select the most interesting association rules:

- Source: user defined knowledge or association rule selected as "new knowledge"
- Confidence level: 5 different values are available to describe knowledge confidence according a domain expert. These values are range of confidence value: 0-20%, 20-40%, 40-60%, 60-80% and 80-100%. We call confidence the probability the consequence of a knowledge occurs when the condition holds.
- Certainty:
  - Triviality: cannot be contradicted
  - Standard knowledge: domain knowledge usually true
  - Hypothesis: knowledge the user want to check

This is an example of knowledge:

KNOWLEDGE 1
Objective='To be paid' $\wedge$ Allowance='Housing Allowance' $\wedge$ Distance='0km' $\rightarrow$ Contact='At the agency'

- Source: user-defined
- Confidence level: 60-80%
- Certainty: Hypothesis

6.2   Ruled-Based Knowledge Base

Knowledge, like interestingness, differs from people and changes over time. That's why our knowledge base is divided into several sets. A main set defines high level and consensual knowledge while subsets allow to define user's knowledge. Since knowledge may differs between experts, the main objective of this knowledge base is to provide the expert some personalized models according his current knowledge.

6.3   Interesting Patterns Extraction

Interestingness definitions. In [14] Silberschatz presents a classification of measures of interestingness and identifies two major reasons why a pattern is interesting from the subjective (user-oriented) point of view:

- Unexpectedness: a pattern is interesting if it is surprising to the user
- actionability: a pattern is interesting if the user can do something with it to his or her advantage

Therefore a pattern can be said to be interesting if it is both unexpected and actionable. This is clearly a highly subjective view of the patterns as actionability is dependent not only on the problem domain but also on the user's objectives at a given point in time [11].

Although unexpected patterns are interesting it's necessary to consider actionable expected patterns. In our approach we deal with actionability using knowledge certainty property:

- If a pattern match a trivial knowledge it isn't actionable since actions concerning trivial knowledge are most likely known
- Since user knowledge define his main points of interest, a pattern matching standard knowledge could be actionable
- If a pattern matches a hypothesis, it is highly actionable

Patterns and knowledge comparison. In this paper we compare patterns and knowledge considering generalization relationships between them. In future works, we will introduce a distance measure which will consider both differences and generalization relation between patterns and knowledge. Liu introduce such a distance measure in [9] to deal with *general impressions*.

We propose an interestingness measure *IMAK* (Interestingness Measure According Knowledge) which consider:

- actionnalibity, using certainty knowledge property
- unexpectedness, using generalization relationships between patterns and knowledge.

At the moment, we don't use a distance measure so we cannot consider patterns that differ partialy from knowledge if there is no generalization relationship between them. However these patterns are interesting and need further treatments. Patterns that are totaly different from knowledge can't be evaluated by *IMAK* measure but they could be interesting since they're unexpected.

Consequently *IMAK* is useful in order to evaluate interestingness of patterns which are comparable to prior knowledge. This measure describe four levels of interest:

- none: uninteresting information
- low: confirmation of standard knowledge

Table 2. IMAK values when pattern and knowledge have similar confidence level

Knowledge Certainty → ↓ Pattern is ...	Triviality	Standard knowledge	Hypothesis
more general	low	medium	high
identic	none	low	medium
more specific	none	low	medium

Table 3. IMAK values when a pattern have the best confidence level

Knowledge Certainty → ↓ Pattern is ...	Triviality	Standard knowledge	Hypothesis
more general	medium	high	high
identic	none	low	medium
more specific	none	medium	high

- medium: new information about a standard knowledge/confirmation of a hypothesis
- high: new information about a hypothesis

Tables 2, 3 and 4 show *IMAK* value according generalization relationship between a pattern and a knowledge, certainty of the knowledge and comparison of confidence level between pattern and knwoledge.

Let's consider the knowledge rule 1, and the two following extracted rules:

EXTRACTED RULE 1
Objective='To be paid' ∧ Allowance='Housing Allowance' → Contact='At the agency' [confidence=20%]

EXTRACTED RULE 2
Objective='To be paid' ∧ Allowance='Housing Allowance' ∧ Distance='Less Than30km' → Contact='At the agency' [confidence=95%]

Rule 1 is a generalisation of the knowledge (see Section 1). But its confidence is lower than knowledge confidence level. Consequently *IMAK* value is "low" since the knowledge certainty is "hypothesis" (ref table 4 column 3 line 1). Rule 2 is also a generalisation of the knowledge. Its confidence is better than than knowledge confidence level. Consequently *IMAK* value is "high" since the knowledge certainty is "hypothesis" (ref table 3 column 3 line 1).

Table 4. IMAK values when knowledge have the best confidence level

Knowledge Certainty → ↓ Pattern is ...	Triviality	Standard knowledge	Hypothesis
more general	none	none	low
identic	none	low	medium
more specific	none	none	low

Now let's consider the rule:

EXTRACTED RULE 3
Objective='To be paid' ∧ Allowance='Student Housing Allowance' ∧ Distance=
'0km' → Contact='At the agency' [confidence=75%]

Rule 3 is more specific than knowledge and its confidence is similar. Consequently *IMAK* value is "medium" since the knowledge certainty is "hypothesis"
(ref table 2 column 3 line 3).

7   Experiments Results

Our approach is based on a toolset, called KEOPS, which allows to manage data
preparation process, mining tasks and visualization step. KEOPS main feature
is to use expert's prior knowledge all along the data mining process. Furthermore, KEOPS simplifies several complex tasks during the knowledge extraction
process. We applied this approach on data of the 'family' branch of the french
national health care system.

In order to evaluate our results we compare extracted models to prior knowledge according to their support, confidence and lift values. That's why we define
confidence gain, *support gain* and *lift gain* in order to visualize statistical information on figures 6, 7 and 8 :

Definition 1 (Measure Gain). *Let R be an extracted rules and let C be a
knowledge. We call a measure gain, the difference between the measure evaluation
on R and C :*

$$MeasureGain(R, C) = measure(R) - measure(C)$$

IMAK measure allows us to select the most interesting extracted rules according
knowledge. Figure 6 shows relative confidence of these rules. On X-axis there are
68 knowledge rules expressed by experts and on Y-axis, for each rule, there is a
vertical bar where :

- the upper point shows relative confidence maximum value for rules compared
  with the knowledge
- the medium point shows relative confidence mean value of all rules compared
  with the knowledge
- the bottom point shows relative confidence minimum value for rules compared with the knowledge

We may observe that generally for each knowledge there exists an extracted
rule with a better confidence value. Furthermore, extracted rules confidence
mean value is often better than knowledge confidence value.

Figure 7 shows relative support of the most interesting extracted rules according IMAK measure. Legend of figure 7 is similar to figure 6 one. We may observe
that generally relative support value is lower than 0. Consequently, extracted

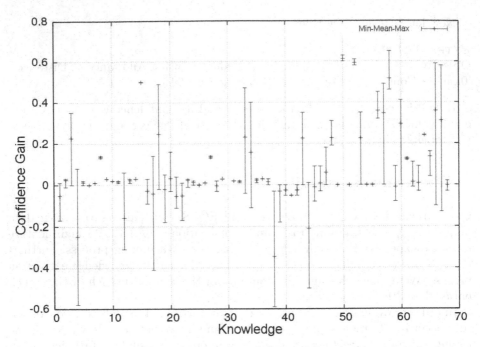

Fig. 6. Relative confidence between knowledge and associated extracted rules

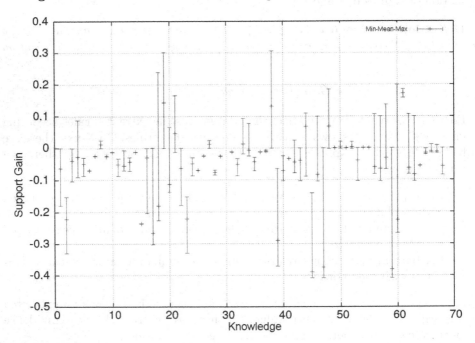

Fig. 7. Relative support between knowledge and associated extracted rules

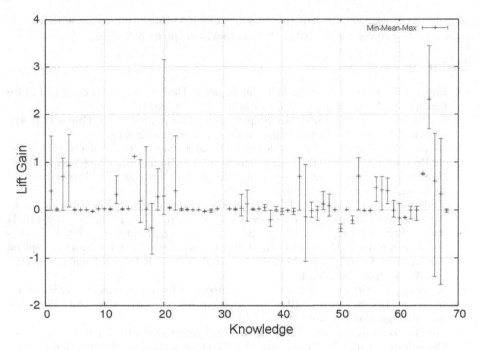

Fig. 8. Niveaux de lift relatif entre les connaissances et leurs règles associées

rules support is lower than knowledge support: these rules are infrequent cases. While some of them have also good confidence and lift, IMAK method catches some rare cases.

Figure 7 shows relative lift of the most interesting extracted rules according IMAK measure. Legend of figure 6 is similar to figure 6 one. We may observe that lift value of knowledge and extracted rules is similar. It's important to notice that expert knowledge has always a lift value greater than 1.

We presented a method which allows to select interesting rules according prior knowledge. Moreover we demonstrate that we extract rare rules (low support values) with good confidence and lift value. Consequently, our approach optimizes statistic criteria and provides some new and interesting knowledge.

8   Conclusion

We gave a global presentation of the new methodology ExCIS for the integration of prior knowledge in a data mining process. This paper shows how a Conceptual Information System (CIS) can improve data-mining results. We presented CIS ontological structures, and we discussed choices for identifying ontology concepts and relations by analyzing existing operational data. Finaly we presented IMAK, an interestingness measure, which evaluate an extracted pattern according to user knowledge. In further works, we'll improve IMAK with distance measure between pattern and knowledge, and we'll add to ExCIS approach mechanisms in order to generalize patterns (process 7 figure 1) before comparison with knowledge and to browse results after this comparison (process 9 figure 1).

References

1. Bard, J.B., Rhee, S.Y.: Ontologies in Biology: Design, Applications and Future Challenges. Nature Review Genetics 5(3), 213–222 (2004)
2. Chapman, P., al.: CRISP-DM - Step by step data mining guide CRoss Industry Standard Process for Data Mining, http://www.crisp-dm.org/
3. Dai, H., Mobasher, B.: Using Ontologies to Discover Domain-level Web Usage Profiles. In: Proceedings 2nd ECML/PKDD Semantic Web Mining workshop (August 2002)
4. Guarino, N.: Formal Ontology and Information Systems. In: Proceedings of FOIS'98, pp. 3–15 (June 1998)
5. Hilderman, R.J., Hamilton, H.J.: Evaluation of Interestingness Measures for Ranking Discovered Knowledge. In: Cheung, D., Williams, G.J., Li, Q. (eds.) PAKDD 2001. LNCS (LNAI), vol. 2035, pp. 247–259. Springer, Heidelberg (2001)
6. Johannesson, P.: A Method for Transforming Relational Schemas into Conceptual Schemas. In: Rusinkiewicz, M. (ed.) Proceedings 10th ICDE conference, pp. 115–122. IEEE Press, New York (1994)
7. Kashyap, V.: Design and Creation of Ontologies for Environmental Information Retrieval. In: Proceedings 12th workshop on Knowledge Acquisition, Modelling and Management (October 1999)
8. Liu, B., Hsu, W., Chen, S.: Using General Impressions to Analyze Discovered Classification Rules. In: Proceedings 3rd KDD conference, pp. 31–36 (August 1997)
9. Liu, B., Hsu, W., Mun, L.-F., Lee, H.-Y.: Finding Interesting Patterns using User Expectations. Knowledge and Data Engineering 11(6), 817–832 (1999)
10. Geng, L., Hamilton, H.J.: Interestingness measures for data mining: A survey. ACM Comput. Surv. 38(3) (2006)
11. Mcgarry, K.: A Survey of Interestingness Measures for Knowledge Discovery. The knowledge engineering review, 1–24 (2005)
12. Pasquier, N., Taouil, R., Bastide, Y., Stumme, G., Lakhal, L.: Generating a Condensed Representation for Association Rules. Journal of Intelligent Information Systems. In: Kerschberg, L., Ras, Z., Zemankova, M. (eds.) Kluwer Academic Publishers
13. Piatetsky-Shapiro, G., Matheus, C.: The Interestingness of Deviations. In: Proceedings of the AAAI-94 workshop on Knowledge Discovery in Databases (1994)
14. Silberschatz, A., Tuzhilin, A.: On Subjective Measures of Interestingness in Knowledge Discovery. In: Proceedings 1st KDD conference, pp. 275–281 (August 1995)
15. Silberschatz, A., Tuzhilin, A.: What Makes Patterns Interesting in Knowledge Discovery Systems. IEEE Transaction On Knowledge And Data Engineering 8(6), 970–974 (1996)
16. Stevens, R., Goble, C.A., Bechhofer, S.: Ontology-based Knowledge Representation for Bioinformatics. Brief Bioinformatics 1(4), 398–414 (2000)
17. Stojanovic, L., Stojanovic, N., Volz, R.: Migrating Data-intensive Web Sites into the Semantic Web. In: Proceedings 17th ACM Symposium on Applied Computing, pp. 1100–1107. ACM Press, New York (2002)
18. Stumme, G.: Conceptual On-Line Analytical Processing. In: Tanaka, K., Ghandeharizadeh, S., Kambayashi, Y. (eds.) Information Organization and Databases, ch. 14, pp. 191–203. Kluwer Academic Publishers, Dordrecht (2000)
19. Tiffin, N., Kelso, J.F., Powell, A.R., Pan, H., Bajic, V.B., Hide, W.A.: Integration of Text- and Data-Mining using Ontologies Successfully Selects Disease Gene Candidates. Nucleic Acids Research 33(5), 1544–1552 (2005)

The Semantic Desktop: A Semantic Personal Information Management System Based on RDF and Topic Maps

Edgar R. Weippl, Markus Klemen, Stefan Fenz, Andreas Ekelhart,
and A Min Tjoa

Vienna University of Technology, A-1040 Vienna, Austria
weippl@securityresearch.at
http://www.securityresearch.at

Abstract. Desktop search tools are becoming more popular; they allow full text searches using inverted indexes. Yet, the amount of locally stored data that they have to deal with is increasing rapidly. A different approach is to analyze the semantic relationships among collected data and thus preprocess the data semantically. The goal is to allow searches based on relationships among various objects rather than focusing on objects' names. This would allow for searches far more sophisticated than those based on full text analysis. We introduce a database architecture based on an existing software prototype that is capable of meeting the various demands of a semantic information manager. This architecture is also capable of storing and querying RDF and RDF schemata. Moreover, RDF is used as a key part of the technology. Therefore, in this scenario, RDF is used not only to enrich the Web with machine-processable semantics, but also to incorporate it into a kind of Semantic Desktop Search Engine. In this paper, we describe the underlying technology of this research project.

1 Introduction

More and more data is accumulating on personal computers these days. People store their journals, time managers, contact data, photos, and other documents on their computers. Despite all efforts, thus far no search tool has been created that allows searches based on semantic connections. What is interesting is that most current approaches focus on enriching the World Wide Web semantically. Our approach focuses in on the domain of a single user who stores and retrieves data on one or more computer systems using semantic enrichment.

Although it is accordingly situated somewhere between RDF-based or Topic Map-based Semantic Web projects, such as, Sesame [8] and and personal lifetime data storage projects, such as, MyLifeBits [13] or SemanticLife [3]the approach and underlying architecture differ fundamentally from either of these concepts.

For retrieval, our approach focuses on the relationships among various local data-objects (such as, photos, e-mails, graphics, and text files) and events (opening a text file, receiving a phone call, sending an e-mail) rather than relying on

M. Collard (Ed.): ODBIS 2005/2006, LNCS 4623, pp. 135–151, 2007.

the names of these objects. Our intent is to allow for more human-like retrieval processes by adding semantic metadata to the data collections. For example, instead of finding a text file based on its name, a semantic search would allow a context-aware query, for instance, *I don't know the filename but I know I created it when I was talking to Jim on the phone about a week ago.*

Our prototype collects raw data from multiple sources such as the operating system's file events or user events from Microsoft Outlook via agents. At the file-system level, we receive data identifying the applications that have accessed (read or written) a particular file. The user can select which applications or directories to monitor, typically these are local office applications and user document folders. For instance, we can store the information that Word.exe has saved a specific file document.doc on the disk at a certain time and date. From Microsoft Outlook we can gather information on emails, contacts, and calendar items. We also store information on the specific computer used (to differentiate between laptops and workstations) and the user ID. Planned are additional data collectors that can integrate incoming and outgoing telephone calls (via CTI or serial printer ports) as well as facsimiles, GPS data, and EXIF[1] metadata from digital camera images.

Based on the vast amounts of data accumulated, a semantic enrichment engine (SEE) is implemented that uses the data and derives information from it to build semantic databases for human users. Clearly, the usefulness of the system as a whole depends on the quality, speed, and versatility of the semantic databases and on the capabilities of the semantic enrichment engine. In this paper, we will focus on the underlying database schema and propose a database architecture that provides the foundation for semantic analysis. There are certain requirements for such a database:

- *Flexibility:* A database for semantic storage must be highly flexible. It must be able to store heterogeneous data from various sources including e-mail systems, file systems, date books, telephones, and GPS modules. Defining new relationships between existing entities will be a common task.
- *Compliance:* The database should be compliant to emerging Semantic Web standards such as RDF or Topic Maps.
- *Backwards compatibility:* All enhancements to the database must be backwards compatible. Modification of the database schema should occur only rarely.
- *Speed:* The database must perform well at high speeds due to the high volume of processed data.
- *Scalability:* The database design should allow for up-scaling of the database with no significant performance loss.

More specifically, our contribution:

- provides an overview of the architecture of our Semantic Desktop Project prototype
- proposes an intuitive and efficient method for storing arbitrary relationships (Section 3.2).

---

[1] http://www.exif.org/

- shows that our database schema is well suited to store both RDF Metadata and Topic Maps (Section 3.3).
- explains why it is more efficient in comparison with other approaches (Section 4).

2   The Problem

An increasing capacity for data storage enables people to save virtually their whole life digitally in various file formats or databases-photos, videos, e-mails, address databases, etc. Available personal programs to store and manage these files usually offer searches either via file system hierarchies or via keywords or full text search (in cases where the file contains text data). *Filesystem hierarchies* not well suited since it is often not possible to make precise attributions to a single, specific folder [11]. *Keywords* are commonly either based on the file name or must be typed in manually. Manual keyword input is cumbersome, time consuming, and subject to the *Production Paradox* [10]—people will simply not do it since they see no immediate advantage. *Fulltext-engines*, on the other hand, are useful for text-based documents only. Integrating photos and music into full-text-based systems is difficult and an area of ongoing research.

Apart from that, people tend to forget names of specific objects. It is often easier to remember the *context* of a situation in which a specific file was created, modified, or viewed, especially with reference to a *timeline* ("I remember I just got an e-mail from Mike when I was working on that document").Semantic enrichment of automated data-gathering processes is a useful tool to complement this human, relational way of thinking, rather than thinking in keywords or tags.

3   The Semantic Desktop Project

At the first phase, Blackman should help the user to scan the computer, queried by Blackman query language (see [12]), for certain data files and an important part for this task is the integration of Microsoft Outlook 2003 and the collection of data hosted there. A big part of information, a user is producing, is located at the e-mail-client and so Blackman works in a first try with Microsoft Outlook 2003, to extract the following elements:

- e-mails
- calendar entries
- contact entries

The extracted data will be saved at database to make a future query- and rule-creation possible. Due to the modular structure of Blackman it is not difficult to integrate further watchers for additional e-mail-clients produced by other vendors than Microsoft. The second part of the Blackman project should monitor the file system and network activity to gather as much user data as possible. An example: If the user is opening a file, Blackman should recognize this, to create an entry of this event at database. This action will be represented by an event which could be enriched with some information like time, location and certain other circumstances at which the file was opened.

In a next step a 'Semantic enrichment engine' should make the collected data useful to the user. The engine should implement certain ontologies which can be used, to enrich collected data semantically, for purposes like 'Personal organization', 'Security', 'Visualization' or any other usage where data of user's behavior is needed.

So how could this data be used to make the organization of user's life much easier?

At this phase of Blackman it is necessary that the user is planning his day, is administering his contacts and is storing his e-mails with Microsoft Outlook 2003. With this precondition Blackman is able to reconstruct what and when the user is doing something, to reconstruct users daily life.

The following listing describes a few sample use-cases to make the ideas above more understandable:

- When the user is participating at a meeting from 10:00 to 12:00 and is working at a certain document for a defined duration it is highly possible that this document has something to do with the meeting. If there is a meeting next week with the same participants and a similar topic, Blackman should collect automatically all relevant documents and make them available to the user before the meeting starts. This would be a use-case for a specific business usage.
- In many companies it is normal that documents, even confidential documents, are sent by e-mail to the desired recipient(s). This could be a security approach for Blackman; the semantic enrichment engine could be implemented in a way that it 'knows' which documents are confidential. There are several ways how Blackman could classify a document automatically as confidential. One possible approach would be that Blackman is looking, when user receives a document, in the address book entries for sender's position within the company. Blackman also looks on the list of recipients which can be found in the header of any e-mail. If, for instance, user's department chief is the sender and the mail was sent only to one person it is highly possible that this document is confidential. From this point Blackman 'knows' that this document is confidential and monitors every action which has something to do with the, as confidential classified, document. At another day the user wants to forward this document unintended to all co-workers, due to analysis of e-mail header and content Blackman will recognize that, and fires up an alarm.

  A different security approach would be the detection of abnormal user activity. Blackman records almost every action taken at users machine. If, for instance, due to a evil worm, abnormal outgoing network traffic is generated, Blackman could block and alert this traffic, to ensure users data integrity and security. Therefore Blackman could be implemented in a specific way, to provide similar functions as a 'Intrusion Prevention System'.

– If Blackman is installed organization wide it is possible to track document changes to enable the creation of a work flow visualization. Not only the work flow within the organization is tracked, due to e-mail monitoring also contacts to external actors are recognized by Blackman and could be merged with the internal work flow. The creator or owner of a document could see what is happening with 'his' document and who sends it to whom.

The surveillance of network- and e-mail traffic enables Blackman also to build up a visualization of social networks.

Recapitulating, Blackman should help the user to organize his data, which could be realized by recording his daily life behavior. Based on automatically or manually created rules the collected data will be enhanced with semantic data to provide, through Blackman, a practical benefit to the user. The whole data gathering process is happening in background, to ensure that the user has not to 'fight' with an additional system on this machine.

The Semantic Desktop project goes far beyond typical full-text analysis search engines by automatically enriching collected data with semantic context that can be used for retrieving it more easily than without this context.

Our prototype was developed in DotNet and Java, and consists of five major development components:

1. *Request Handler:* The Request Handler consists of various modules to process external data sources. It is explained in more detail in Section 3.1.
2. *Semantic Storage:* Storing semi-structured, highly interconnected data requires data models that take these characteristics of semantic environments into consideration. In this paper, we thoroughly explain how our approach satisfies those requirements.
3. *Semantic Enrichment:* Semantic Enrichment is crucial for the usability of a semantic information management system.
4. *Querying Interface:* The Querying Interface is another critical element. We develop an interface that is compatible with OWL while still providing easy and secure access to the specific needs of a personal desktop information system.
5. *Client Application:* Currently, we have a prototype client in use written in DotNet. A Java-based Webclient is planned after the DotNet client is released and sufficiently stable.

In this paper, we will focus on the Semantic Storage development area. We introduce an improved database schema and provide examples for how concepts and relationships are stored among the databases. We then show (Sections 3.3 and 3.4) how both RDF and Topic Maps can be stored efficiently.

3.1   Request Handler

We distinguish four types of data input channels: (1) *Native Data Pipes* (2) *XML-based data exchange* (3) *SOAP request broker* (4) *HTTP request broker*

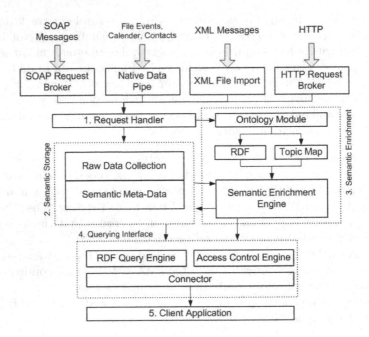

Fig. 1. System architecture: data is collected from various sources and stored in the raw data collection. Subsequently, the semantic enrichment engine (SEE) analyzes the data based on ontology guidelines and RDF or Topic Map based rules and adds links between recorded data items.

Native Data Pipes: Currently we have three data pipes. (1) Outlook Data Pipes for Microsoft Exchange Server, to access calendar entries, contacts, and e-mails; (2) an OS File Data Pipe, which is hooked directly into the I/O system of Windows 2000/XP/2003; and (3) a Network Traffic Data Pipe, which monitors network traffic for both URL requests and for tracking visited websites.

XML-Based Data Exchange: We use this module for research studies comparing Unix-based semantic data collection with the Windows-based variants. The idea behind this is to develop universally valid semantic statements, which may be used in both Windows-based and Unix-based environments. We are currently collecting data for semantic analysis on both Windows and Unix machines and we expect interesting results within the next half year.

SOAP Request Broker and HTTP Request Broker: Both modules are in the early stages but will facilitate the networking of various client machines to build a unified personal information management system. This will be an important part of the project since more and more users are working on more than one computer and therefore could profit from a system that would allow the interconnection of these devices.

3.2   Semantic Storage

Our prototype, first described in [17], is based on an architecture that uses relational databases. Tables are not linked to others *directly* with foreign keys or by using $n : m$ intermediary tables, but instead, via a single, generic association table referred to as the *link table*.

In the classical schema, adding an $n : m$ relationship between two tables requires creating a new intermediate table to resolve the $n : m$ relationship into a $1 : n$ and a $1 : m$ relationship. Our approach is to merge these intermediate tables into one link table that stores all relationships centrally.

The advantages of our approach are:

1. In contrast to classical E-R approaches, any relationship can be added without schema modifications. This allows for easy performance of operations within transactions.
2. Tables and indices can be clustered to improve the speed of *join* operations with the central link table. In the classical model, multiple $n : m$ relationships exist, therefore, cluster optimizations are far more difficult and less efficient.
3. Our approach permits retrieval of relationships from the link table without accessing the data dictionary. Since the data dictionary is vendor specific, the classical approach requires modifying the application for each database system.
4. If n entities exist and $n : m$ relationships are to be established between all entities, the number of additional tables is $O(n^2)$, whereas our approach is $O(1)$. Of course this applies only to new relationships, not to new tables.

Detailed explanations on the advantages can be found in [17].

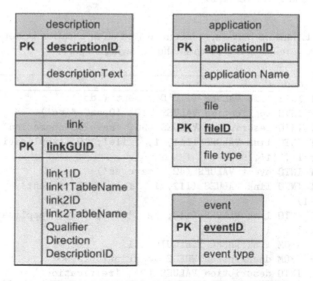

Fig. 2. The database schema to store the information as given in Table ref1

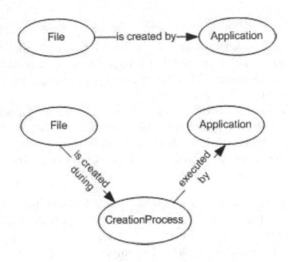

Fig. 3. Reification

Figure 2 shows a simple database schema. Table 1 contains the SQL statements of the following example. A new file type, Document (.doc), is created with OpenOffice. An optional description is added and a relationship between the two topics is established (steps 1–4). In the same way, occurrences can be linked to topics.

Reification is an important process for a semantic system. It is highly probable that a semantic analysis module will initiate reification while processing collected raw data. Steps 5-10 in Table 1 show how reification (Figure 3) can be easily implemented using our schema.

Table 1. A relationship between a document and an application is stored (steps 1–4). An example for a reification is given in the following steps.

Step	SQL Command
1	`INSERT INTO file VALUES (1, 'Document (.doc)')`
2	`INSERT INTO application VALUES (10, 'OpenOffice')`
3	`INSERT INTO description VALUES (90, 'save as operation')`
4	`INSERT INTO link VALUES (111, 1, 'file', 10, 'application', 'assocrl', '1', 90)`
5	`INSERT INTO event VALUES (42, 'save as')`
6	`INSERT INTO link VALUES (112, 1, 'file', 42, 'event', 'assocrl', '1', 91)`
7	`INSERT INTO link VALUES (113, 42, 'event', 10, 'application', 'assocrl', '1', 91)`
8	`DELETE FROM link WHERE linkGUID=111`
9	`DELETE FROM description WHERE descriptionID=90`
10	`INSERT INTO description VALUES (91, 'reification')`

Our concept differs from to other approaches (Section 4) by using separate tables to store different types of entities but one central link table for all relationships. The data-centric approach, which we also refer to as the "classical" method, uses one table for each $n : m$ relationship. The structure-centric approach stores everything in one table (such as an RDF triple store).

The advantage of our approach as compared to the data-centric approach is that we require fewer changes of the database schema during normal database operations. Adding a new type of relationship—a very common operation in semantic systems-requires no schema modification. The structure-centric approach has the same advantage but suffers from a different drawback. Since everything is stored in a single (or very few) tables, this table will quickly become very large and thus be slower to access. Numerous self-joins, which will be required, also have a negative impact on performance. Moreover, only general purpose database indexes (B-trees) can be used. Our approach, in contrast, permits defining Bitmap and Function-based Indexes[2] that are extremely efficient in some cases and completely useless in all other cases.

3.3   Storing Topic Maps

Even though the structure-based approach is slower during retrieval, it may make sense to implement it in a very dynamic environment where new entities, new relationships, and even new types of relationships are created frequently. These characteristics typically apply to semantic environments such as RDF or Topic Maps. Modifying the aforementioned link-based architecture, we show that the relational storage model as proposed by [19] can be optimized in several ways helping to improve the performance and reduce the complexity of the database schema.

First and foremost, we can reduce the number of tables used without the loss of data or metadata (Figures 4 and 5). By using `qualifiers` in the link table we can combine tables such as `basename`, `sortname`, `dispname` and `topname` into one table called `name`. The qualifier attribute in the link table contains information on whether the name is used as basename, sortname, etc.

Following the XTM standard[3] we also no longer need the table `facet`. The link that connects topics and associations stores the `association` role as `qualifier`, rather than in a separate table. In the same way we can avoid separate tables for `fvalue`, `locationstype`, `nonconforming` and `cassign`.

Since 'everything' is a topic we do not need to explicitly store this information in a table. Instead, we propose creating a view that contains all the information (create view ... as select from ... UNION selection from ...).

The main difference between RDF and Topic Maps that is relevant to storing information is that RDF only supports relationships between two entities-RDF uses nodes and arches to build graphs of concepts and relationships between them. This makes storage much easier and the simplest approach is to store RDF triples in the form (s, p, o) (subject, predicate, and object) [2].

---

[2] Using an Oracle database.

[3] http://www.topicmaps.org/xtm/1.0/

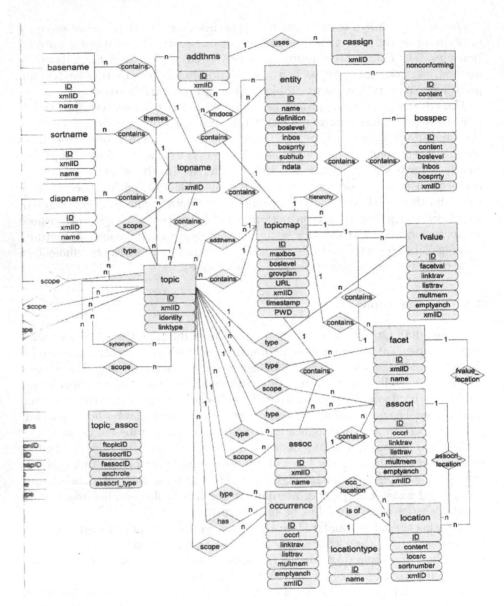

Fig. 4. Storing Topic Maps in an RDBMS [19]

3.4   Storing RDF

However, RDF can be stored similarly to Topic Maps by using either the "pure" link-based approach (Section 3.2) or modifying it in a way that is analogous to what we showed for Topic Maps. All four major differences between RDF and Topic Maps can be handled by the link-based approach:

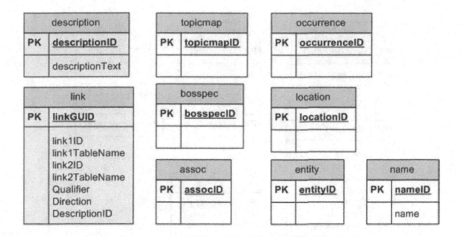

Fig. 5. By storing all relationships in the `link` table together with a qualifier, fewer tables (compare to Figure 4) are needed but all advantages as described in [19] are retained

1. In RDF, relationships can only be established between two resources whereas Topic Maps support relationships among any number of topics. The link table supports an arbitrary number of links.
2. In RDF, relationships are directed and only valid for one direction. In most cases this requires creating a redundant second and inverse relationship. In the link table, an attribute is used to store the direction.
3. In contrast to Topic Maps, RDF does not support scopes, which makes it difficult to create large ontologies by combining existing smaller ones. If scopes are required, a table (scope) needs to be added. By linking the appropriate scope via the link table, scopes can be handled easily.
4. In RDF, reification is necessary if additional information must be attached to a relationship at a later time. This is not necessary for Topic Maps since everything is already reified. As shown previously, reification can be performed efficiently with our database schema.

Figure 6 shows how RDF data as described in [8] can be stored in our database structure. For efficiency and design considerations, we use five entities: Domain, Range, Resources, Property, and Class. All other entities described by [8] can be mapped by appropriate links and qualifiers in the `link` table.

Rather than using a table `subPropertyOf` (Figure 7) we qualify the recursive relation of property accordingly. `Literals` and `labels` are mapped to descriptions, the `type` to the qualifier of the `link` table and `namespaces` are implicitly defined in the description. `Range` is a qualifier of `domain`; `subClassOf` is mapped to `class` with a qualified recursive relation. The link table corresponds to the `triples`.

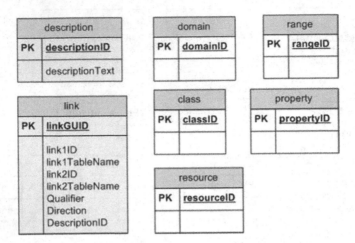

Fig. 6. Our database schema can store RDF (such as shown in Figure 7) independently of Topic Maps in the same schema

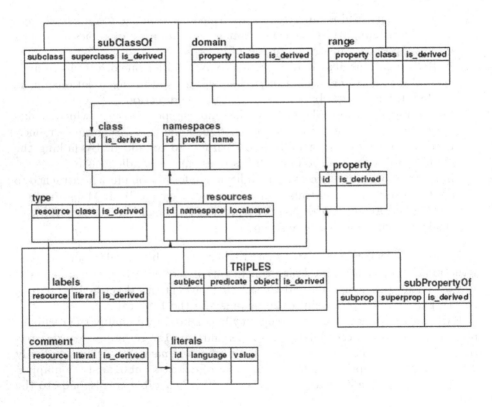

Fig. 7. The original RDF storage schema as proposed by [8]

4   Evaluation of Other Storage Concepts

In this section we look briefly at three systems that store personal information and strive to provide semantically enriched retrieval capabilities. For more details please refer to [18]. We then look at existing solutions (data-centric approach and structure-centric approach) to organizing a semantic data store.

4.1   Storing Personal Digital Information

Vanevar Bush's vision of the Memex [9]—a paper cited nearly universally when writing about semantically enriched information storage-provides the base for projects, such as, Microsoft's *MyLifeBits* [13] or the *SemanticLIFE* project [3] build. The authors aim to create a personal digital storage that records all of an individual's documents, emails, photos, videos, etc.

MyLifeBits focuses on storing digital content in a database; unlike SemanticLIFE its primary aim is not a semantic enrichment of the stored data. Instead, MyLifeBits relies on future improvement of search engines and desktop search solutions. The focus of SemanticLIFE is to build ontologies and discover relationships between existing data items.

Haystack [1] is a platform to visualize and maintain ontologies. The system is designed to flexibly define interactions and relationships between objects. Focus lies on the quality of the retrieval process and not on storing data.

While both systems inherently address issues of storing ontologies, they do not focus on an efficient storage concept. MyLifeBits assumes that the MSSQL Server will provide all the needed functions without providing details on the database schema used.

4.2   Data-Centric Approach

One approach also known as a data-centric approach is often mentioned in the context of mapping XML documents to relational databases [15,5,6,16]. In terms of ontologies, the process can be described as follows:

The first step is to identify the types of concepts and their properties that are to be stored in the ontology. Then, these types of concepts are mapped to corresponding tables in a traditional RDBMS, with the previously identified properties being the fields of the tables. Finally, the instances of the classes can be inserted into the tables as rows, with one row representing one instance of a concept. This procedure is the same for subjects, relationships, and all other data model entities defined by the respective standard.

In addition, several 'auxiliary' tables are needed to keep track of whether a certain table maps to a subject or to a relationship, etc. This leads to a situation in which the database is actually split into two 'virtual layers': the virtual 'schema layer' consists of the auxiliary tables that keep track of all classes in the ontology, whereas the virtual 'data layer' contains the tables created as instance containers for specific classes.

Such a data-centric approach was, for instance, originally followed by the Sesame ontology framework [7,8] in conjunction with a PostgreSQL database. Figure 8 shows the setup of the Sesame data centric object-relational mapping.

There are two advantages that can be exploited with the data-centric approach. First, query answering as well as inserting, removing, and updating instances of classes is extremely inexpensive and straightforward, as there is virtually no difference to traditionally designed databases. All manipulations concerning instances are, in effect, nothing more than executions of the data manipulation commands that are natively provided by all RDBMS.

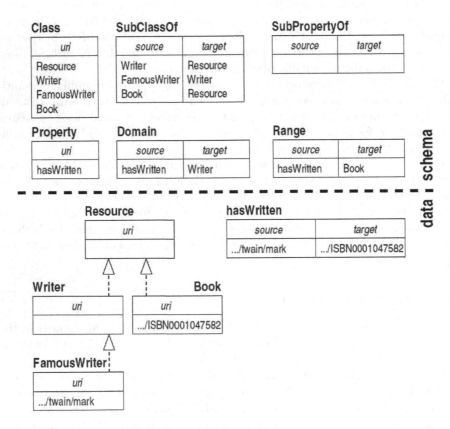

Fig. 8. Data-centric approach of Sesame [7]

Second, some RDBMS, such as, PostgreSQL, offer built-in object-relational features that can be used directly for modeling class-subclass relationships, etc. PostgreSQL databases offer, for instance, the possibility to create subtables that are connected to their parent tables through transitive relationships. This enables creating a table for a certain class and corresponding subtables (for subclasses of that class). The same is true for properties and subproperties, accordingly.

The main drawback of the data-centric approach is that changes to the class hierarchy in an ontology are extremely expensive, as they require creating new entities in the database. For every new class (and also subclass) that is to be inserted into the ontology, a respective table has to be created, even if only a small number of instances are present. This means that changes to the class hierarchy always require the performance of data definition commands, which are expensive in almost any RDBMS.

4.3   Structure-Centric Approach

The second approach is also known as structure-centric and is equally popular among Topic Map and RDF implementations. As is the case with the data-centric approach, persistency is provided by a traditional RDBMS, but usually without requiring object-relational features. In contrast to the first approach, the key idea here is to map the finite number of data model concepts to corresponding structures (tables) in the relational database. Again, the process has also been described for XML documents [15,5,6,16], but additionally, has been specifically implemented for both Topic Map and RDF applications.

As shown in detail in Section 3.3, the Topic Map data model offers a small number of built-in concepts, such as, Topic, Association, Occurrence, Scope, etc., whose properties are well defined. In contrast to the actual classes and instances they represent, the number and design of these built-in concepts are static (as they are standardized). Therefore, it is a straightforward task to create corresponding structures in a RDBMS and map the concepts to these structures in such a way that in the end there is one table for all topics, one table for all associations, etc. Various examples of this implementation for Topic Maps exist, e.g., [14,19].

With respect to RDF, the data model basically consists of statements only, with each statement including a subject, an object, and a predicate. This means that for a naive approach, only one single table (with three corresponding text fields containing the respective URIs or literals) is needed to express a complete RDF graph. Due to the layout of their tables, databases configured this way are therefore commonly referred to as triple stores. They are certainly a very elegant solution for ontology persistence and are probably one of the main reasons that RDF/OWL has gained significant popularity among ontology developers. Also, many variations and improvements over the naive approach are available, mainly for achieving high levels of scalability.

The first advantage of the structure-centric approach is its ability to allow for inexpensive, frequent changes of instance data as well as of schema information (class hierarchies). Since all assertions, including hierarchical relations, are broken down to the level of single statements, it is not necessary to make any artificial distinction between 'schema layer' and 'data layer.' This not only allows for the representation of frequently changing ontology hierarchies, but also for efficient incremental incorporation of large datasets, since no structural changes of the underlying database schema are required.

The second advantage of structure-centric ontology representation is commonly reported for dedicated triple stores, but also applies to Topic Map representations. Due to the fixed, rather simple architecture of the database, scalability optimizations are easy to apply, enabling the efficient storage of millions of concepts and relationships.

One main disadvantage of the structure-centric approach (in the case of RDF triple stores) is encountered when retrieving statements for answering ontology queries. In order to evaluate a condition that does not directly address the URIs or literals of the statements to be retrieved, the table containing the statement triples has to perform one or more self-joins, an operation that is expensive for large datasets [15,4]. Such large datasets must be seen as occurring frequently, as an ontology's entire information is stored within a single triple table. It is, therefore, common for such a table to contain millions of triples, and these triples must be compared to one another, often several times, depending on the nature of the query to be answered. Although various optimization efforts attempt to limit the negative effects of storing triples in a single table, in general, a lower level of performance in answering queries is to be expected as compared to the object-relational approach.

5   Conclusion

The Semantic Desktop Project aims at bringing the potential of RDF, Topic Maps, and Semantic Technologies to users' desktops. The goal is to develop a semantic personal information management system based on standards, such as, RDF, XTM and DAML+OIL/OWL, which assists users by automatically enriching collected data with semantic metadata.

Some important milestones are already in beta-testing, allowing performance tests and research regarding the querying of semantic statements. In this paper, we presented the current status of the project and proposed our improved method for storing ontologies in a relational database, which allows changes of hierarchies and relationships between tables to be added easily without schema modification.

The advantages of our approach are:

1. The modifications require no data-definition language (DDL) statements that cannot be executed within a transaction.
2. Tables and indices can be clustered to improve the speed of joins with the central link table.
3. Our approach is vendor-independent as no metadata on relationships need to be retrieved from the data dictionary.

In addition, we showed that Topic Maps and RDF can be stored efficiently using our database schema.

Acknowledgements

This work was performed at the Research Center Secure Business Austria funded by the Federal Ministry of Economics and Labor of the Republic of Austria (BMWA) and the federal province of Vienna.

References

1. Adar, E., Karger, D., Stein, L.A.: Haystack: Per-user information environments. In: Proceedings of the Conference on Information and Knowledge Management (1999)
2. Agrawal, R., Somani, A., Xu, Y.: Storage and querying of e-commerce data. In: Proceedings of VLDB 2001, Rome, Italy (2001), http://www.vldb.org/conf/2001/P149.pdf
3. Ahmed, M., Hanh, H.H, Karim, S., Khusro, S., Lanzenberger, M., Latif, K., Elka, M., Mustofa, K., Tinh, N.H, Rauber, A., Schatten, A., Tho, N.M, Tjoa, A.M.: Semanticlife — a framework for managing information of a human lifetime. In: Proceedings of the 6th International Conference on Information Integration and Web-based Applications and Services (IIWAS) (September 2004)
4. Alexaki, S., Christophides, V., Karvounarakis, G., Plexousakis, D.: On storing voluminous RDF descriptions: The case of web portal catalogs. In: ICSFORTH. Proceedings of the 4th International Workshop on the the Web and Databases (2001)
5. Bourret, R.: Xml-dbms, http://www.rpbourret.com/xmldbms/readme.htm
6. Bourret, R.: Mapping dtds to databases. Technical report, XML.com (2001), http://www.xml.com/lpt/a/2001/05/09/dtdtodbs.html
7. Broekstra, J., Kampman, A., van Harmelen, F.: Semantics for the WWW. In: Sesame: An Architecture for Storing and Querying RDF Data and Schema Information. MIT Press, Cambridge (2001), http://www.cs.vu.nl/~frankh/postscript/MIT01.pdf
8. Broekstra, J., Kampman, A., van Harmelen, F.: Sesame: A generic architecture for storing and querying rdf and rdf schema. In: Horrocks, I., Hendler, J. (eds.) ISWC 2002. LNCS, vol. 2342. Springer, Heidelberg (2002)
9. Bush, V.: As we may think. The Atlantic Monthly 176(7), 101–108 (1945)
10. Carroll, J.M., Rosson, M.B.: Paradox of the active user. ch. 5, pp. 80–111. Bradford Books/MIT Press (1987)
11. Dourish, P., Edwards, W.K., LaMarca, A., Lamping, J., Petersen, K., Salisbury, M., Terry, D.B., Thornton, J.: Extending document management systems with user-specific active properties. ACM Trans. Inf. Syst. 18(2), 140–170 (2000)
12. Ekelhart, A.: The blackman project: Collecting and querying semi-structured data for the 'semantic desktop'. Masterthesis, University of Technology Vienna, Vienna (2005)
13. Gemmel, J., Bell, G., Lueder, R., Drucker, S., Wong, C.: Mylifebits: Fulfilling the memex vision. In: ACM Multimedia '02, pp. 235–238. ACM Press, New York (2002)
14. Kiyakov, A.K., Simov IV, K., Dimitrov, M.: Ontomap: Ontologies for lexical semantics. Technical report, OntoText Lab, Sirma AI EOOD (2001), http://www.ontotext.com/publications/ranlp01.pdf
15. Kuckelberg, A., Krieger, R.: Efficient structure oriented storage of xml documents using ordbms. Technical report, RWTH Aachen (2003)
16. Mittermeier: Naiv nativ. iX 42(8) (2003)
17. Weippl, E.R., Klemen, M., Linnert, M., Fenz, S., Goluch, G., Tjoa, A M.: Semantic storage: A report on performance and flexibility. In: Andersen, K.V., Debenham, J., Wagner, R. (eds.) DEXA 2005. LNCS, vol. 3588, pp. 586–595. Springer, Heidelberg (2005)
18. Weippl, E.R., Klemen, M.D., Raffeiner, S.: The Semantic Web for Knowlege and Data Management: Technologies and Practices. In: Improving Storage Concepts for Semantic Models and Ontologies. Idea Group, USA (2007)
19. Widhalm, R., Mück, T.: Topic Maps: Semantische Suche im Internet. Springer, Heidelberg (2002)

Author Index

Lecture Notes in Computer Science

Sublibrary 1: Theoretical Computer Science and General Issues

For information about Vols. 1– 4475
please contact your bookseller or Springer